BACKPACKER
The Magazine Of Wilderness Travel

Trekker's Handbook

BACKPACKER

The Magazine Of Wilderness Travel

Trekker's Handbook

**STRATEGIES
TO ENHANCE
YOUR
JOURNEY**

Buck Tilton

THE MOUNTAINEERS BOOKS

THE MOUNTAINEERS BOOKS
*is the nonprofit publishing arm of The Mountaineers Club,
an organization founded in 1906 and dedicated to the exploration,
preservation, and enjoyment of outdoor and wilderness areas.*

1001 SW Klickitat Way, Suite 206, Seattle WA 98134

BACKPACKER
The Magazine Of Wilderness Travel

33 East Minor Street
Emmaus, PA 18098
800-666-3434
www.backpacker.com

Published simultaneously in Great Britain by Cordee, 3a DeMontfort Street, Leicester, England, LE1 7HD

Manufactured in Canada

Acquisitions Editor: Cassandra Conyers
Project Editor: Kathleen Cubley
Copy Editor: Joeth Zucco
Cover and Book Design: The Mountaineers Books
Layout Artist: Jennifer LaRock Shontz
Illustrator: Jennifer LaRock Shontz
All photographs by the author unless otherwise noted.

Cover photograph: *Trekking on Mount Sunapee, New Hampshire* © Rob Bossi
Frontispiece photograph: *The journey goes ever on. Wind River Gorge, Wyoming.* © NOLS/
    Deborah Sussex

Library of Congress Cataloging-in-Publication Data
Tilton, Buck.
  Trekker's handbook : strategies to enhance your journey / Buck
Tilton—1st ed.
      p.—cm.
Includes bibliographical references.
  ISBN 0-89886-957-9 (pbk.)
1. Hiking—Handbooks, manuals, etc. I. Title.
  GV199.5.T55 2003
  796.52—dc21
                              2003012496

Table of Contents

Part 4
Coming Home   144

Part 1
Introduction

> "This is the stone, drenched with rain,
> that marks the way."
> *Santoka*

Zen and the Art of Trekking

It had started, as it always does, with a dream. Now, from the rutted dirt of a parking spot just off the rutted dirt of an access road, I shut off the car and the sound drifted away into tremendous silence. The trailhead stood beneath my booted feet, and from the silence I heard—or felt—the Siren call that only the possibility of vast wilderness creates. I was elated. I would return in 10 days, days to wander aimlessly and pointedly, days to forget things and remember things. The wild world was mine—and I was its.

Thinking back to those moments, and many others like them, I ask myself, from the familiarity of my desk chair, what motivates a person to step out on a trek. "Trek" here meaning not necessarily 10 days, but probably close to a week at least, a hike of 30 miles or more. "Trek," reports an old dictionary pulled from my bookcase, means "to go on a journey." Whatever the length of days, whatever the distance, that definition satisfies me. And it is not only the geography of the earth that draws me out, although that is a major factor, but also the geography of the mind and the heart. I am traveling to see the sights, yes, but more to see ever deeper into myself and into this thing called life. The mountains, the lakes and rivers, the infinite sculpted majesty of canyon country beckon me—but what will I feel on those rocky flanks, on those seldom-trod shores, in those sandstone depths. In a world dominated by something other than humans, you are left, more than any-where else, with yourself.

Like life, it is true that the destination remains relatively meaningless compared to the steps taken to move toward that destination. As masters of Zen casually state, to live totally in the moment is to live most fully. And how better to be in

It's time to start making plans to take the journey, to live the dream (NOLS/Deborah Sussex).

the moment than contemplating the next foot placement on rough terrain, rummaging through the food bag for dinner, sucking up water with a filter, or considering the view from a possible campsite. The goal is to be here and now, and here and now is the only place I am. To trek, for me, has come to be synonymous with living—and there is my motivation.

Perhaps you cannot identify with the view from my chair. Perhaps you are motivated by an opportunity to do something different, or something that demands self-reliance, or something that simply physically challenges you. Those, too, are considerable but lesser motivations for me. Perhaps it does not matter much the why at the start of a trip, but it will matter at the end. And then you can sit contemplatively and answer for yourself.

Let the record show, I do believe that the longer the trip into wilderness the greater the opportunity to walk deeper into yourself. There is a passage the human spirit goes through that only opens after an extended period of time in uncluttered wild places. How much time? It varies, I reckon, with the individual depending on how thickly "civilization" has coated you. I have trekked for as long as 52 days in Idaho and 62 days in Wyoming, dependent on my backpack and a cache of food, and it is an incomparable experience. At the end of the passage though, however long, you become increasingly a part of the wildness instead of an observer, an intruder. And when you see the wholeness of human and wild, when the myth of separation drops away, you see much deeper and more accurately into the very essence of being.

It starts now with your dream. You have decided to take your first long backpacking trip, or another long backpacking trip, the culmination, perhaps, of years of dreaming. Where will you go—forests, deserts, tundra? It is your dream. But for a moment a desperate thought may struggle with elation for control of your brain: How do I know I am ready? We can agree, I think, because you have opened this book, that you want to trek, whatever the days or miles. For you, and once again for me, the journey goes ever on.

The Adventure of America

Before getting into the how-to of trekking—and admittedly and without embarrassment, my philosophy of trekking—I feel constrained to say a few words in defense of America. It is simply a magnificent country, and nowhere, absolutely nowhere on this planet, will you find such environmental extremes: the cactus-strewn expanses, the jagged heights, the pulsing glades, the breezy grasslands, the tumbling rivers, the ever-white majesty above tree line, the dripping and shadow-clad forests, the waves of sand, the indescribable variety of wonder that is Alaska. And nowhere will you find among the masses of humanity such devotion and endeavors to preserve and protect the natural splendor. Our national park system, the first of its kind on earth, offers trekking opportunities encompassing any imaginable diversity. Yellowstone, Yosemite, Denali, Isle Royale, Great Smoky Mountains, Zion, Shenandoah, Haleakala—the names explode with magic and invitation. Our National Wilderness Preservation System, also the first of its kind on earth, offers trekking opportunities far beyond the limits of a human lifetime. Wrangell–Saint Elias, Gates of the Arctic, Frank Church–River of No Return, Weminuche, Absaroka-Beartooth, Popo Agie, Cabeza Prieta, Death Valley—the list extends to more than 650 designated wildernesses. Our long trails, the first of their kind on earth, provide trekking opportunities of virtually endless magnitude: 138 miles of Arizona's General Cook Trail, 140 miles of Arkansas's Ozark Highlands Trail, 254 miles of Kentucky's Sheltowee Trace, 800 miles of the Florida Trail, 2000 miles of the Appalachian Trail, 2600 miles of the Pacific Crest Trail, 3000 miles of the Continental Divide Trail. There are more, and more are being planned. I sit drowning in the tragic brevity of one's human existence—and exulting at what lies within reach of a couple of tanks of gasoline.

A Note About Safety

Safety is an important concern in all outdoor activities. No book can alert you to every hazard or anticipate the limitations of every reader. The descriptions of techniques and procedures in this book are intended to provide general information. This is not a complete text on trekking technique. Nothing substitutes for formal instruction, routine practice, and plenty of experience. When you follow any of the procedures described here, you assume responsibility for your own safety. Use this book as a general guide to further information. Under normal conditions, excursions into the backcountry require attention to traffic, road and trail conditions, weather, terrain, the capabilities of your party, and other factors. Keeping informed on current conditions and exercising common sense are the keys to a safe, enjoyable outing.

The Mountaineers Books

PART 2
Before You Go

> "To know what we do not know
> is the beginning of wisdom."
> *Maha Sthavira Sangharakshita*

What came first, a long-forgotten human once asked, the chicken or the egg? More recently a trekker, probably also human, asked: What comes first, the destination or the information? As with the poultry dilemma, the answer is the same: It does not matter. If you know where you want to trek, start gathering info. If you have not chosen a destination, gather info about places to go, choose, and keep on gathering info. The unexamined trek is not worth taking.

Gathering Information

A successful trek, one from which you return safe and well and happy and busting at the seams to start your next one, begins with information. How much information you gather will depend on three factors: how much time you have, and, ideally, you have started the process months in advance; how much information you truly need, a sum of such variables as experience, environment, and eagerness to learn; and how smart you are, since those who get into trouble tend to be those who fail to gather enough of the appropriate information.

Unless your memory is phenomenal, it does not make much sense to gather valuable data and not write it down. The result is a well-conceived plan and a checklist that changes with the season of the year, the geography of the area, the never-ending development of new equipment, and the obtuse fluctuations of your mind.

Planning will increase your enjoyment of a trek. Indeed, the anticipation planning creates becomes for many an integral part of the joy and wonder. And planning helps prevent the guess-what-I-forgot syndrome. Such forgetfulness can be

Gathering information builds the foundation on earth for your castles in the sky (NOLS/ Fredrik Norrsell).

life-threatening if the forgotten item is necessary for survival, or something others in your group were counting on you to bring, say the wine-filled bota. The research, the plan, the list are an indispensable part of the journey. Grab a pen and paper, and start building a foundation on earth for your Thoreau-ish castles in the sky.

Interviews

There is no greater predictor of success than success. There is no more valuable source of general (and sometimes very specific) information than people who have already done what you are planning to do. Where do you find those people? If they are not numbered among your friends and acquaintances, check out a local hiking club or the staff at a nearby outdoor store. Go to the Internet, to local land managers, to organizations that support and promote wilderness travel.

The Internet

Millions of people and sources of information are linked via computers, and the answer to almost any question lies literally at your fingertips. You can use search engines, contact individuals and organizations, even order relevant books, high-tech gear, and a wardrobe of outdoor clothing. You can

Questions to Ask

▲ How do I access the starting point? What is the road like? Are there times when I just cannot get there? If the ending point and starting point are not the same, what will I find at the end point?

▲ What is the terrain like? What are the trails like?

▲ What is the worst weather I can expect?

▲ How far from trail's head to trail's end? How long did it take you to walk that distance?

▲ Where did you camp? Was there water available?

▲ What did you carry? Did you wish for something you did not have?

▲ If you were going to do the same trek again, would you do anything differently?

subscribe to news bulletins, join discussion groups, and ask any question of just about anybody. The *Backpacker* website, *www.backpacker.com*, gives you immediate access to people, places, and mountains of news and advice including detailed evaluations of gear and clothing. There are billions of other websites (see Appendix A for a few) where you can often find data ranging from daily weather forecasts for specific wildlands to a list of the birds you might see there. You can download and print much of what you find. It is completely amazing . . . and it is frightening.

Books

Guidebooks, how-to books, and sometimes narratives are essentially extended interviews with people who have been there and done it (see Appendix B). Some trekkers swear by them, and some swear at them. They may contain valuable information about distances, terrain, weather, water sources, campsites, even glimpses of history and peeks at wildlife. They can add a huge amount of knowledge to your plan, but even if a book was published or updated recently it could have been months, sometimes many months, since it was written and specific information may have changed. It is best to compare the information in books to other sources.

You do not always have to buy the book. Borrowing is an age-old practice, and libraries have made a business of it. Libraries may also be sources of informational CDs, magazines, and online databases. Of course if you own a book, you might decide to tear out relevant pages and pack them along.

Local Land Managers

Backcountry rangers who work for the U.S. Forest Service (USFS), the Bureau of Land Management (BLM), the National Park Service (NPS), and other government agencies are often the most up-to-date source of information about current conditions in a specific area. They may be able to direct you to or even provide, sometimes free of charge, other sources of information including maps. And they will be able to inform you about required permits or local regulations.

Organizations

From small local backpacking clubs to the massive national and international organizations that protect and defend wilderness, you will find people who want, or at least are willing, to help you plan your trek. A phone call or an email can put you on the trail to loads of information (see Appendix A).

Maps

A few days ago I sat with a friend hunched over a map of a section of the Arctic National Wildlife Refuge, a bird's-eye view of the site of the next trek on my dream list. Will I be able to cross that river? Will I be able to ascend that peak? Will caribou in the thousands be grazing over that vast stretch of tundra? Conduct your interviews and read your books, but nothing conjures up the magic of an intended trek more than poring over the contours and colors of a map! On a map you can "see" the geographical journey before you step out on it.

Maps tell you distances, elevation gains and losses, and maximum elevations gained. Maps reveal hidden lakes and the extent of cloud-shrouded glaciers. Maps show water holes in the desert, mysterious ruins in dark canyons, and where the shadowed forest gives way to alpine treelessness. Maps set fire to the imagination.

USFS maps and BLM maps, although they give you an overview, do not typically provide enough detailed topography to serve the specific needs of the trekker. In some areas, however, such as national parks and well-managed wilderness areas, where trails are well-maintained, an agency map might suffice. Better, in most cases, to rely on U.S. Geological Survey maps with the best detail provided by 7.5-minute quads in 1:24,000 scale. On the downside, USGS quads are often old, maybe very old, and fail to show current trails and other signs of human intervention. Commercial maps are increasingly available and increasingly accurate, and many treks can be planned with one or more of these. You can also download topo maps from the Internet. Computer software allows you to create your own custom maps that you can spice up with notes and Xs marking the spots. Topo map CDs are available from National Geographic and DeLorme. (See Appendix A.)

Outdoor Education

When the student is ready, the teacher will come. Or, in some cases, you might go to the teacher. For more than thirty-five years, for instance, the National Outdoor Leadership School (NOLS) has been offering extended educational trips into the wild outdoors, trips lasting from a couple of weeks to a semester. NOLS, and similar schools of outdoor education, can prepare you fully to plan and take your own treks (see Appendix A).

The map becomes the outline of the dream (NOLS/Deborah Sussex).

Permits and Regulations

Some trekworthy areas, national parks for instance, often require permits. Sometimes you may need a permit to hike, and sometimes you may need a permit to camp at specific sites. Some permits require a request in advance, some can be acquired at the trailhead, some are not free, and all are worth checking into prior to standing before a tight-lipped ranger two miles from your vehicle.

Regulations may also apply to specific areas. Some trails may be closed in order to protect wildlife or to allow regeneration resulting from overuse. Regulations may limit the size of a party and/or the use of open fires. A few regulations may be in force to protect you, such as those governing how you should camp in bear country. All regulations should be known in advance. They may seem inconvenient, but they are not arbitrary, and they help keep the promise of wildland remaining wild.

Communication

At the home of a friend one night, during a visit to Colorado, the phone rang. Another friend was calling, from the summit of Mount McKinley. I had stood where the joyous mountaineer was standing, but even the few years that separated our summits marked a vast increase in technology. No means to communicate in such a way from such a remote spot existed when I was there.

You cannot assume that your cell phone, ground-to-air radio, or other semimagical communication device will work on your trek. You could be out of range, or deep in a topographical "black hole" without the possibility of making contact, or far from the aerial path of aircraft. On the plus side, such tools can give you the needed edge to succeed when an emergency threatens limb or life. On the negative side, they can give you a false sense of security that would be much better replaced with the skills and gear to manage emergency situations confidently and with self-reliance. Such tools can also, and often have been, used inappropriately, initiating a rescue, and putting others at risk, when it was not necessary.

The choice of whether or not to carry electronic communication devices is entirely personal. If you do carry, say, a radio, you must also carry the skills to use it, the knowledge of when to use it, and an understanding of its limitations.

> "It does not matter how slowly you go
> so long as you do not stop."
> *Confucius*

Route Planning

Route planning, at least here, refers to the specific trail or trails you plan to hike, and how you will connect trails, should you wish to do so, that have no junction.

Your chosen route, primarily a result of the information you have gathered, will develop from variables including how much time you have to see what you want to see with the energy available from your body and mind.

Distance and time. A general rule governing trail mileage suggests a relatively fit hiker with a reasonable weight on her or his shoulders can cover about 2 trail miles an hour. An average hiker with a full load on moderate terrain, says another rule, can cover 5–10 trail miles per day. But then rules, said Paul Petzoldt—the late, and wise, founder of NOLS—are for fools. What matters is what you can do, and only experience can finally answer that question. If you have not been under a pack recently, you will want to plan for shorter distances on your first day or two out to allow break-in time for your muscles and boots. And if the trek is a long one, you will want to take a rest day at least once per week. But . . . .

Terrain. "Hard" trails take more time than "easy" trails. "Hard" might mean rough or steep ground. Rough terrain—bogs, talus, boulders, river crossings, and just about anything off-trail—can cut your miles-per-hour in half. An elevation gain of 1000 feet will add an hour to your estimated travel time compared to the same distance on flat earth.

High altitude. Coming from sea level, or thereabouts, you will notice the strain of thinner air starting as low as 5000 feet elevation. Almost everyone, except for the well-acclimatized, will move at a slower pace by the time they reach 7000–8000 feet. Plan your distances and times accordingly. From 8000 feet up, and especially above 10,000 feet, you are in the range of high altitude illnesses, and a slower pace may prevent serious complications (see "Health and Safety" in On The Trail).

Campsites and water sources. How far you travel each day needs consideration, perhaps more than anything else planning-wise, as to where you will pitch your tent each night and refill your water bottles. Little blue lines on maps do not always guarantee flowing water. Here your best info usually comes from a land manager who knows the route or someone who has recently trod those miles.

Linking Trails

As a novice trekker I remember studying a map and saying, "Okay, we'll hike to the head of the canyon, climb out, cross the mesa, and drop down into the next canyon." I should have studied a better map. A week later I stood at the rim of the "next canyon" and looked down vertical cliffs with absolutely no means of descent. It took a day of waterless rim-walking to find access to the bottom. Yes, there is adventure in stepping out into the unknown, but successful trekkers more often are found among those who trace their routes on detailed topographical maps.

> ### Success Tip
>
> New to trekking? Start on the small end of big. Take a weeklong hike, then a two-week hike, before heading out on a monthlong journey.

And they talk to someone who has made the link before. The map may show a ridge with a slope of acceptable inclination, but standing at its foot you find impossible scree that sends you two steps back for every one step up and an overhanging cornice of sun-baked snow at the top.

Loops vs. End-to-End Treks

In well-trailed areas you can sometimes stay on pathways that join each other for the entire trek and end up at your starting point—not often, but sometimes. Places such as the Fossil Ridge Wilderness of Colorado entice you to hike up a trail to a beautiful lake, cross an easy low ridge to another lake, and hike down another trail to the same parking lot from where you started. A more typical, and adventurous loop involves a day or two of traveling cross-country, climbing a mountain, wading a river, hitting a second trail, and ending up where you began. These trips, in a sense, could be called perfect loops. An imperfect loop, if you want to call it that, leaves you several miles from your car. Not a big deal if you do not mind walking the road back to your vehicle.

If more than a "few" miles separate trail's end and trail's head, you have traveled an end-to-end hike. Then you have the additional logistical step of arranging for transportation when you walk out tired and exhilarated (see "Transportation Considerations," below).

I do not number among those who think it problematic to turn around at the end of several days and travel back over the same ground. A trail traveled in the opposite direction never fails to seem fresh and new to me—well, almost never.

Transportation Considerations

For end-to-end hikes, the safest bet is to leave a car at the trail's end before you, assuming there are at least two of you, start out from the trailhead. Second best is to arrange for someone to meet you at the end. Accepting responsibility to meet trekkers at the grand finale of a trek is a noble thing since you might be hours, or sometimes a day or so, behind schedule.

Another transportation consideration involves the condition of the access road or roads. The rule here: Do not make assumptions. Call whoever is responsible for the road to learn if the road is maintained, if a high-clearance vehicle is required, if there is a parking place, how changes in weather—rain, snow—will affect the road, and how safe the parking lot is from vandalism.

> **Success Tip**
>
> When you have a route chosen, the distance and time estimated, and the possible or probable campsites and water sources picked, you have an itinerary. Write it down—and leave a copy behind with someone you trust.

You don't know what the trailhead looks like unless you ask (Alan Bauer).

> "Imagination is more
> important than knowledge."
> *Albert Einstein*

The Map of Dreams

At the heart of every route plan lies a map, a map as accurate as you can find. With the information gathered and processed, you can see the route on paper, either in your mind and, even better, highlighted in brilliant yellow or neon orange. On the trail it will always be handy. Protect the map in a clear plastic bag, and fold it to reveal each day's intended journey so you do not have to expose it to the elements to read it. The map will be the outline of your dreams.

When to Go

"When" might depend on numerous variables including when the boss will let you off, when your favorite trail companions are available, or when the mood strikes. But in the ideal trekking world, you go when you are most likely to experience the things you want to experience, such as flights of monarch butterflies, or when the weather promises, or at least suggests, it will be as perfect as possible.

Summer swarms of mosquitoes fill the air thicker than molecules of oxygen in Gates of the Arctic National Park. By late August, early September, the nights freeze, doing away with the bugs, but the days usually remain warm and inviting. I trekked into the park in late August and early September, returning home deeply satisfied and bite-free.

> "To know others is wisdom,
> to know yourself is enlightenment."
> *Lao Tzu*

Trail Companions

When the trails—or lack of trails—are chosen, when the distances are measured, when the season draws near, you may have not yet made what is arguably the most important decision: Who will you trek with?

Within the past week a friend of mine returned home after 16 days of solo trekking along a spine of northeastern mountains. His report: All went well and the fun factor stayed high. One of his reasons for the happy report: No one else to slow him down, or speed him up, or complain about the food or the weather or his body odor. There is a sweet pleasure to solo trekking—but you lose a few significant advantages when you are alone. You have to carry all the gear and food, you risk having no one to immediately respond if you are injured, and you have no one to hang out with on the trail or in camp. My longest solo trek, 9 days walking near the Idaho-Montana border, went exceedingly well. But I missed having someone to talk over the day with, and I have decided that the touches of wonder I feel are increased when someone I care about shares them. A solo trek may provide an incredible experience, but, for physical and emotional safety, first build an experiential base of trekking with others before choosing to head out alone.

On the other side of the trekking coin, as suggested above, few things, if any, can ruin a trip faster than a companion whose personality irritates you more than a horde of whining mosquitoes. The code of the trail demands that you suffer the rotten trail companion when you would rather slip off quietly into the night, just as you must support the companion who is physically overchallenged by the trail.

So . . . if you have not yet, you soon will appreciate that the longer the trek, the greater the importance of selecting companions thoughtfully. Your best chance of having everything work out companionably is to travel shorter distances with this person or these people prior to setting out on a trek. How about a shakedown weekender with the proposed group before everyone commits to the trek?

The Ideal Companion

1. Someone who shares your desire to trek
2. Someone who travels at a similar pace
3. Someone who enjoys the wilderness experience as much as you do
4. Someone who accepts the risk
5. Someone who has helped plan the trip
6. Someone you like a lot
7. Someone willing to carry heavier loads than you

Man's Best—and Worst—Friend

Dogs. Most trekkers stand firmly either for or against them, with few straddling the canine fence. Whatever your stance, there are a few facts worthy of consideration:

- ▲ Dogs are not immune to trail hardships, including sore feet, heat, cold, insects, and dehydration. To take a dog and not attend to its health is irresponsible at least and inhumane at worst.
- ▲ Dogs are not permitted on many trails.
- ▲ Dogs may chase wildlife—reducing your experiential opportunities and possibly inflicting irreparable harm—which in turn, may chase the dogs and bring the wildlife back to you.
- ▲ Dogs do not follow the guidelines of Leave No Trace (see "Leave No Trace" in On the Trail), so you have to do it for them.
- ▲ Dogs are often subject to specific rules and regulations that become your responsibility.
- ▲ Dogs tend to become a source of friction between you and other hikers by being overly friendly or overly aggressive.

Wildlife

From small fur-balls to majestically antlered monarchs, wild animals add much of the wonder to a wildland experience. They can also subtract things as bothersome as a bag of oatmeal or as significant as an arm or leg. Your information-

Enjoy your journey. Allow others to enjoy theirs (Alan Bauer).

gathering spree should leave you with knowledge related to the importance of hanging food out of reach of mice and raccoons, and whether or not you should bear-proof your camp (see "Campsite Selection" in On the Trail). Wildlife encounters tend to impact the animals more strongly than they impact us. Wild animals habituated to finding food packed in by humans become "problem" animals, and the problem invariably becomes one for the animals. Do not intentionally or unintentionally feed wild animals. Frightened animals sometimes flee their known territory, at times leaving their young behind—both to the detriment of the.animals. If animals alter their behavior because of your presence, you have disturbed them. Keep your distance. Enjoy your journey, and allow them to enjoy theirs.

Gear

For more than a decade I have taken part in testing gear and clothing at *Backpacker*, and this is what I can tell you: There is a lot of great stuff out there. But you want it to work, and you want to like the way it works. Beyond that good, better, and best apply to little else except how products work for you. And that said, we can look at things to consider.

Shelter

Shelter means protection—for you and, if large enough, your gear. Protection from wind and water. Protection from biters and stingers. Protection from cold.

Bivy bags. The smallest and lightest way to go, I have taken short treks—in the one week range—with a bivy bag and nothing else for a roof. A good one can withstand a heavy rainfall, even a foot of snow—both of which should be something of a surprise if all you have is a bivy bag. A good one has netting that zips over the opening, to keep creepy crawlies and fierce fliers out, and a tent pole designed to hold the thing off your face. A bivy bag works for me when the weather is forecast to be fair to middling because I do not want to lie in that enclosed space waiting out a storm, wondering if the rain is soaking into everything else that I stuffed into a garbage bag.

Tarps. I have been out for a month and more with a tarp for shelter. A tarp was my first shelter, and I crawl back underneath one often. In addition to being light and simple, the art of setting up a tarp appeals to me. They can be adapted to almost any geography, even a treeless beach where I used sea kayak paddles as poles. The drawbacks, of course, are numerous—no bug netting, no floor, no storage pockets, nothing to stop a hard wind from curling underneath. If you do not mind bugs, dirt, and wind, and perhaps a driving rain now and then, take a tarp. But take some extra cord—trees do not always grow exactly the correct distance apart. Note: Bivy bags and tarps can be combined and still leave you with less weight than most tents. Bivy bags and tarps can weigh as little as 2 pounds while tents range from 2.5 to 8 pounds or more.

Tarps can be set up in any terrain.

Tents. In most cases, excepting extremes of cold, a tent is a luxury item. But then there is nothing wrong with luxury. As in all things, luxury is relative—the more luxury, the more the cost and weight. If you plan to trek only in summer, you can, however, get a good tent without too much cost and weight. A three-season tent (spring to fall) will suffice for most trekkers on most treks, at additional cost and weight. Only the hardy winter trekker needs to consider the fourth season— and the typically great increases in cost and weight.

For any tent, think about these important things:

- How much floor space does it include? Will it fit you, a companion, and most of your gear? Or is body space enough?
- Is there enough headroom?
- Will the shape help toss wind aside? Aerodynamically rounded sides stand up better to high wind.
- How many poles does it require? More poles mean more stability—and more weight.
- Will the design allow for adequate ventilation? Two doors usually provide excellent ventilation—and more cost and weight. One door and a vent or two may be enough.
- Does it have adequate reinforced points to stake it out in heavy weather? A taut tent repels wind and water better.
- Does it have a rainfly that reaches almost to the ground? A fly is a must, but a short fly may allow water to work its way inside.
- Does the door have mosquito netting with a separate zipper? Many nights you will want the netting up and the fabric down for ventilation.

Luxury . . . for a few additional pounds (NOLS)

Then you can think about these luxuries:

▲ In addition to better ventilation, two doors provide easier access.

▲ Two-way zippers on doors and netting are much handier.

▲ A large vestibule gives you extra storage space and cooking space in wet and wind.

▲ Storage pockets inside the tent allow for better organization.

▲ The easier a tent is to set up, the more you will enjoy setting it up.

Packs

You probably already own a pack. Before deciding if you need another one for trekking, ask yourself two questions about your current pack: Is it comfortable enough? And is it big enough to carry everything?

Comfort. Like a suit of well-made clothing, a pack, first and foremost, should fit. To know that it fits, you have to try it on. The shoulder straps of an internal frame pack should attach to the frame 2–3 inches below the top of your shoulders. You want the top of the frame to reach no more than about 2–3 inches above your shoulders (or your headroom will be compromised). The hipbelt should be centered over your hip bones, and the padded part of the belt should not meet over your middle when the belt is firmly snugged up. The bottom of the pack should not fall much below the hipbelt.

A critical step in choosing a pack that fits is choosing a knowledgeable dealer who can help you. The pack needs to be matched to your height and weight, shoulder width and torso length, and perhaps even your gender. The highest quality packs will have a suspension system that adjusts, and the initial adjustments should be made before you leave the store.

Your pack must fit your body and hold everything you need snug enough to prevent shifting of the load (NOLS/Tom Bol).

Some people prefer external frame packs. They allow you to stand a little straighter, they let cooling air flow over your back on warm days, and they generally cost less. But you will have to compromise balance and your ability to move smoothly over rough terrain unless you choose an internal frame pack. I prefer an internal frame and, to narrow the field, I look for several important options:

▲ A strong, well-padded hipbelt that carries the weight easily. You should be able to shift 80 to 90 percent of the burden onto your hips, putting the workload on your legs instead of your back and shoulders.

▲ A lot of compression straps to secure the load. These straps will allow you to prevent shifting of the pack's contents, an especially important consideration when you are packing smaller loads into a larger pack.

▲ A stable harness system with load-stabilizing straps. Stabilizing straps help you to shift the weight of the pack from one body part to another. These straps at your shoulders can be loosened to shift more weight to your hips, or tightened to shift the weight more forward and onto your shoulders.

▲ A top pocket that detaches and converts into a fanny pack for side trips.

▲ Durable, water-resistant material.

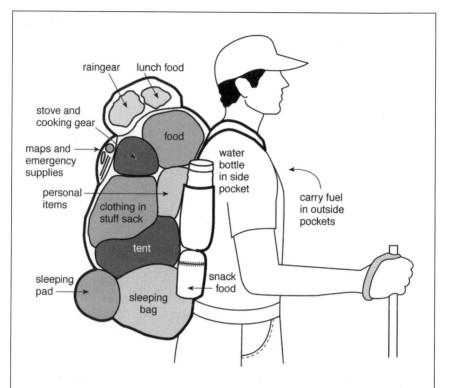

Pack Like a Pro

At 40 pounds, a fully loaded backpack can wear you down or strain your back if not loaded correctly. Packing smart starts with a good fit. Have your outdoor retailer fine-tune the strap adjustments for your torso and expected load.

Consider the terrain, too: On level ground, put the weight up high and cinch the pack in close to your back: on boulders and through rough brush, relocate weight low to help your balance. Always distribute weight equally side to side.

▲ Water, snacks, fuel, maps, guidebook, flashlight, pocketknife, first-aid kit, raingear, pack cover, and other emergency supplies all go in external pockets.

▲ Food (your heaviest category) rides high and close to the body. Cooking gear below that for convenience.

▲ Clothing deep inside, in stuff sacks or sealable plastic bags.

▲ Sleeping bag inside lowest compartment.

▲ Sleeping pad, inside plastic bag, strapped on outside, high or low as you like.

▲ Depending on the configuration of your pack and the weather, the tent can go inside or outside.

▲ Color coding your stuff sacks, memorizing your packing plan, and sticking to it will eliminate confusion about where items are stored.

▲ Detachable, external pocket options to increase your access to oft-needed items and your ability to lose a bit of weight on shorter treks.

▲ For women, consider a pack built especially for your frame.

Capacity. Here, as in most things, your choice is relative. Going as lightweight as possible means, for instance, you do not need as big a pack. You may, in fact, be wise to gather all the other gear and clothing you intend to carry, and then find a pack that holds everything. Of course you may be even wiser to choose a pack of reasonable size and carry no more than it will hold. Time will tell.

If you like numbers, a vast 6000-cubic-inch-plus capacity pack is a moving van for multiweek trips. A midrange pack (4000–5000 cubic inches) will provide enough space for weeklong trips. A slim 2000–3000 cubic incher is more of a weekender, but it can work for an extreme go-lighter.

If you buy it, you will fill it. Choose a pack that holds everything you need—but not everything you could possibly carry (NOLS/Tom Bol).

Packing the Pack

1. Everything that you think you might want on short notice needs to be accessible. You do not want an extended search for your lunch, camera, raingear, or the toilet paper. Items like your sleeping bag and tent can be buried deep.
2. Nothing with sharp or hard edges should be placed where it can jab into your back.
3. The load should be balanced so it rides evenly on your center of gravity. The heavier items ride best close to your body. Otherwise you tend to be pulled backwards. Whether you pack the heavy gear high or low depends on personal taste as well as terrain. Packing the weight high creates less strain on the spine but makes you a little tippy—not a problem when a trail provides relatively easy walking. Packing the load low is a bit harder work because it interferes with your stride, but it gives you more steadiness when the going gets rougher. Overall the heavier items in your pack ride easiest level with your shoulder blades or a smidge lower.
4. A well-packed pack has the load snuggly fitted so it does not shift around, throwing you off balance when you least expect it and most need it.
5. Place small items together in a stuff sack to prevent chasing them around when you want them.

Sleeping Bags

With literally hundreds of sleeping bags to choose from, picking one might first seem an insurmountable obstacle. An obstacle, maybe, but certainly not insurmountable. Here are a few things to consider:

▲ **One sleeping bag will not suffice in all weather conditions.** Manufacturers make summer, winter, three-season, and other types of bags for a reason: a comfortable sleep for you no matter the weather.

▲ **Check the weather forecast again.** Moisture would suggest a synthetic, quick-drying, works-when-damp bag. In the cold and dry, I use a fluffy down bag that packs small and holds body heat in extremes of cold.

▲ **Your choice of bag needs to work for you.** The manufacturer will make claims, your friends will extol the wonders of their choice, but your body works in its own mysterious way. My body makes heat with ease, and I fall asleep warmly while listening to the chatter of teeth from the bag next to mine when both of us are sleeping in the same type of bag.

▲ **The trial-and-error technique of choosing a bag works.** See if you can rent or borrow a bag you are thinking about buying, and sleep in your backyard or near your car one night before heading out a long way from home.

Before a shopping trip learn a bit of sleeping bag lingo:

Temperature rating. This tells you how cold it can be outside your bag and still allow you to stay warm inside. As the rating goes down the price goes up. Unfortunately, the rating acts as a guide only. No absolute standard exists, and you might feel cold in a bag rated to keep you warm. But any bag rated around 20 degrees F will usually provide comfort for spring, summer, and fall. Bags rated above 20 degrees seldom work for most people except on warm summer nights. Bags rated to or below zero work for most people in winter. You only need a well-below-zero rating when you are headed out or up into extremes of cold.

Shells and liners. Sleeping bags have an outer shell and an inner lining. Shells and liners need to protect you against wind and some water, and they need to resist ripping. At the same time they need to "breathe" to allow your body moisture to escape during the night. Ripstop nylon is relatively windproof, a little water resistant, strong, and breathable. It makes a fine shell, especially if you sleep in a tent or bivy bag. Waterproof, breathable fabrics, such as Gore-Tex, cost more but make an excellent shell especially if you plan to sleep tentless. Nylon taffeta is softer than ripstop, breathes well, but is poorly resistant to wind and water. It works well as a liner.

Insulation. Down-filled bags have the best warmth-to-weight ratio, stuff into smaller spaces, and cost more than synthetic-filled bags. Synthetics are generally easier to maintain in the field, drying quicker and working better than down when they are damp.

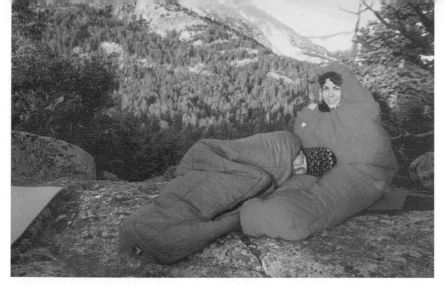

Your bag needs to fit your body and hold in enough body heat to keep you sleeping comfy (NOLS/Tom Wright).

Construction. If the insulation is sewn into pockets to keep it from shifting around, cold can creep in through the seams. Well-made bags are baffled with interior walls that overlap to prevent exposed seams.

Shape and size. Sleeping bags fall loosely into three configurations. Mummy bags are narrow at the feet, wider at the shoulders, and taper from the shoulders to an insulated hood. Mummy bags snug around your body like a cocoon to maximize heat retention, stuff smaller than other shapes, and provide less sleeping room. Rectangular bags are squared at the corners, provide plenty of tossing and turning room, and let your body heat rush out into the night. They are heavier than mummies, take up more room in your pack, and are seldom chosen by backpackers, climbers, and skiers. Semirectangular bags fall in between. Without an insulated hood, however, a semirectangular bag will be little if any warmer than a rectangular bag.

Before buying a bag, get in, zip it up, and roll around so you are assured that you're choosing a bag that fits. Extra room means extra air space your body has to heat up, but extra room may mean a more comfortable sleep, and in winter it provides space for keeping a water bottle or boot liners warm.

Sleeping Pads

Seriously dramatic innovations in sleeping pads deserve a standing ovation, and I would provide one if I was not so comfortable lying down. Even if your sleeping bag keeps you excellently comfortable from the air, you will be miserable from the ground on a poor pad.

Self-inflating pads. Most of the innovations have been in these mattresses. Open the valve and relax while the air rushes in. You will probably want to send in a couple of breaths to firm it up, but the result is maximum comfort. Available in different widths, lengths, and thicknesses, I prefer, well, maximum comfort. The extra weight is worth it—a full-length, standard, self-inflating pad averages 2.5 pounds while a full-length, closed-cell foam pad averages 1.5 pounds. And the extra cost is something I am willing to pay. If you choose one with a non-slip surface, you will not find yourself half on the ground in the morning—or worse, during a cold night. On the downside, they can spring a leak, but the best ones come with a repair kit. And covers are available for these pads that add additional protection for the pad and snap up into a chair for camp lounging.

Closed-cell foam pads. Virtually indestructible, these pads are also light in weight and relatively comfortable—compared to sleeping without a pad. As with self-inflating pads, they will not absorb moisture, they cost much less than self-inflating pads. They do a fair job of insulating you from cold ground.

Open-cell foam pads. The least expensive and the least comfortable, they soak up water and will not give it back easily. You will have to be terribly short of money to consider one.

Repair Kits

No matter how durable your gear (or clothing) a longer trip means a greater chance of having something fall apart, burst open, or rip. To be prepared, pack a small repair kit. You can buy a commercial repair kit, made for the trail, and adapt it to your special needs—or you can construct your own. A basic repair kit could include the following:

1. **Duct tape.** If it cannot be fixed with duct tape, it probably cannot be fixed. You do not need the whole roll. Pull off a few yards and re-roll it or wrap it around a water bottle or trekking pole.
2. **Mechanical wire.** A short piece can make pack repair easier.
3. Sewing kit. A small one allows quick stitching up of torn clothing.
4. **Parachute cord.** A piece 20 feet long or so almost always seems to come in handy for emergencies such as broken boot laces.
5. **Small repair kits** specific to gear such as stoves and sleeping pads.

Accessories

Into the category called "accessories," we can lump all the small stuff needed—or wanted—on a trek. Some have already been discussed, and some wait to be discussed. Here they are simply listed. Your list of accessories might be longer or shorter.

▲ Map and compass
▲ Repair kit
▲ Stove, fuel, and cookware (including utensils)
▲ Cup and/or bowl
▲ Waterproof matches/lighter
▲ Knife or multipurpose tool

- ▲ Flashlight or headlamp and extra batteries
- ▲ Sunglasses
- ▲ Water bottles and a means to disinfect water (such as a water filter or iodine tablets)
- ▲ Medical supplies
- ▲ Toiletries: toothbrush, toothpaste, etc.
- ▲ Camera and film
- ▲ Journal and pen
- ▲ Book to read
- ▲ Watch
- ▲ Binoculars
- ▲ Altimeter

> **The Ten Essentials**
>
> Do not leave home without something for:
> 1. Navigation (map and compass)
> 2. Sun protection (sunglasses and sunscreen)
> 3. Insulation (extra clothing)
> 4. Illumination (headlamp or flashlight)
> 5. First-aid supplies
> 6. Fire (firestarter and matches/lighter)
> 7. Repair kit and tools (including knife)
> 8. Nutrition (extra food)
> 9. Hydration (and water disinfecters)
> 10. Emergency shelter

Clothing

Your garments are your first line of defense against the elements, your most intimate shelter. Looking good may be important to you, but function needs to take priority.

How We Lose Body Heat

To understand the need for clothing, and how to choose the best trekking clothing, you need to understand how the human body loses its life-sustaining heat. Four principles govern heat loss.

Conduction. The first principle arises from nature's desire to create a balance in all things, in this case a heat balance. Whenever your skin comes in contact with a warmer surface, heat moves away from the object and warms your skin. And vice versa. Any surface you touch that is colder than your skin draws heat from you. The greater the difference in temperature, the faster the heat transfer. Step barefoot into a snow bank, and you almost instantly feel the heat leaving your feet. Clothing needs to create a protective, insulating barrier between your skin and anything you might touch that will conduct heat away from you.

Convection. The second principle describes heat lost by way of air or water movement. Your body constantly maintains a thin layer of warm air next to your skin. Wind slicing through your clothing tears away that thin layer that your body immediately replaces. In a high wind you can lose a substantial amount of heat in a short period of time. Dip your hand into a cold, rushing stream to remind yourself how fast water movement can strip heat from your body. You need windproof clothing to prevent convective heat loss.

Radiation. The third principle refers to infrared heat loss from a warmer object to a colder object. Exposed skin radiates a significant amount of heat into the surrounding environment. Since the blood vessels in your head do not constrict much when exposed to cold, heat literally blasts out of your exposed head on a wintry day. So covering your head allows body heat to be transferred to keep you warmer overall. Feet cold? Put on a hat! Your outdoor wardrobe needs to include adequate clothing for all parts of your body, especially your head and neck, in order to reduce radiant heat loss to a minimum.

Evaporation. The fourth principle addresses the escape of heat through the vaporization of moisture, forming the major source of acute body heat loss. Breathing, the inhalation of cool air and the exhalation of air warmed and humidified by your body, accounts for up to one-third of evaporative heat loss. On a hot day the evaporation of sweat from your skin keeps you from overheating. Pour on a little water, and evaporation cools you even faster. On a cold day the evaporation of sweat or water can suck a tremendous amount of heat out of your body. Clothing needs to allow sweat to exit without vaporizing and taking body heat with it. Ideal clothing needs to keep rain or snow from adding moisture to your skin at the same time it allows sweat to exit.

Understanding Clothing

Designer jeans and cotton sweatshirts are fine for strolling the local mall and may keep you adequately protected on a warm, cloudless summer day on the trail, but bring on a sudden storm and that same outfit can become a major source of discomfort. With an understanding of how your body loses heat, your next concern should be choosing clothing made of the best material for use outdoors.

Walk into any store that specializes in outdoor clothing and get ready for a deluge of choices in materials with high-tech names and labels promising a long list of wonderful performances. Relax. Almost all fabrics used in the construction of outdoor clothing, with relative advantages and disadvantages, fall into three categories: cotton, wool, and synthetics.

Cotton. Few people would argue that cotton ranks as the most comfortable fabric next to your skin. Because cotton breathes well, it allows perspiration to escape easily into the air. Cotton also absorbs a lot of water that increases evaporative heat loss. You have probably stood outside at some point in your life in a wet tee shirt and felt the heat rushing out of your body. Cotton, therefore, rates as an excellent choice for hiking in desert regions in the daytime in the summer. Cotton's tendency to cool you rapidly makes it an extremely poor, and often dangerous, choice for cold environments. Cotton works efficiently as a thermal conductor, which means it does not work well as insulation against cold. Three words to remember when considering cotton clothing in winter: Cotton can kill.

Wool. Wool has been worn for centuries by people around the world who spend time outdoors. It offers vast advantages over cotton. Wool fibers, being heavier and coarser than cotton, conduct heat poorly, which means they provide excellent insulation. Wool keeps much of its ability to insulate even when wet. Unprocessed (virgin) wool dries much faster than cotton because it retains oil from the sheep who sacrificed their "clothing." You can wring water from wool clothing, put it back on, and wear it all day without losing much body heat. And if the rain stops, it will dry while you wear it.

More durable than cotton, wool does have its negative side. It tends to be heavy and bulky compared to cotton, and it requires more care. Most wool, for instance, shrinks when washed in hot water or left in the dryer. Some people cannot stand the feel of it next to their skin. Those people will be happy to know that some new wool clothing has been manufactured to be comfortable against the skin.

Synthetics. Synthetics are petroleum products, and they are used to make caps and socks and everything that covers your body in between. Synthetics, in simple terms, are made from plastic woven into thread that is woven into clothing. They fall generally into three classes: undergarments, midlayer garments (sweaters, jackets, vests) often referred to as pile or fleece, and outer-layer garments usually called shells. Synthetic fibers (and sometimes feathery down) are stuffed into synthetic shells to make parkas for extremes of cold. Synthetics conduct little heat, even less than wool, making them the best choice for staying warm. Synthetics absorb almost no water, and actually transport moisture away from your skin, a process referred to as "wicking," making them the best choice for staying dry. They are lighter than wool, compress better than wool for easier packing, and stand up fairly well to hard use.

In the minus column, synthetics, being plastic, melt at relatively low temperatures. You can ruin a good pair of synthetic gloves picking up a hot pot. Unless you purchase special wind-blocking fleece, synthetics allow icy breezes to blow through freely. And synthetics tend to hold onto bad odors such as those produced by a sweaty body.

Hot Weather Clothing

Naturally, you are not going to worry as much about maintaining body heat in warmer weather. In fact, you might be most comfortable if you dress—in shorts and a tee shirt—to shed as much excess heat as possible. In extremes of heat, however, you may find you will feel better wearing lightweight trousers and a long-sleeved shirt that provide protection from the heat of the sun.

> **Success Tip**
>
> Go prepared for the worst possible conditions you can expect in your area of travel.

Hot weather clothing, in general, should be thin and loose fitting to allow cooling air to circulate around your body. Remember what desert dwellers usually wear—billowing robes. Loose-fitting clothing also prevents biting insects from reaching your skin, and light-colored clothing seems to attract fewer insects than dark clothing. Light-colored clothing also reflects the sun's heat while dark clothing absorbs sunlight and increases the chance of discomfort.

A wide-brimmed hat is strongly recommended. Such a hat protects your head, face, and neck from heat and sunburn. A wide-brimmed hat allows you to drape mosquito netting over your head and keep it off your face, ears, and neck. If you cannot part with your baseball cap, wear a bandanna under the cap, allowing it to hang down over your ears and neck in the tradition of the French Foreign Legion.

Your summer pack should contain raingear and a stocking cap—even in desert environments known for intense heat—since wind and temperature drops are not uncommon, especially at night. And a summer rain can make you miserably cold even if the temperature remains the same.

Cold Weather Clothing

Much wisdom lies in a simple adage: "When dressing for the cold, dress like an onion." Three lighter layers of clothing are enormously better than one heavy layer. Multiple layers, like the layers of an onion, allow you to control how much body heat and moisture you retain near your skin (see "How to Wear Cold Weather Clothing," below). Staying dry equates with staying warm, and staying warm equates with staying comfortable. Note that when you go shopping for clothing you may need to buy outer garments in larger sizes in order to have them fit over layers underneath.

A long-sleeved undergarment top, synthetic or synthetic/wool blend, provides the best layer next to your skin. If the garment has a collar, turtleneck or zip-neck, you have added warmth if you need it. Tops with a zip or snap front that opens to a V allow you to partially ventilate the garment. A long-legged undergarment bottom, synthetic or synthetic/wool blend, should go on as your first bottom layer. When you wear this garment, you should wear no other underwear bottom. Some people prefer standard underwear beneath long undergarments, but if you are such a person, remember those skivvies are likely to be cotton. Take them off when you start feeling chilled.

As a midlayer upper garment, a synthetic vest is an excellent choice. A vest adds warmth to vital body areas while allowing great ventilation and complete freedom of movement. Even with a vest, sweaters, wool or synthetic, are important midlayer upper garments. In "warmer" cold weather, wear a light pile sweater. In colder weather, wear a heavy pile sweater in addition to the light one. Trousers, wool or synthetic, are best as midlayer lower garments. Loose-fitting trousers work better by providing more comfort and insulation, and by not sticking to your skin if they get damp and freeze.

For the outer layer, cold weather demands at least a synthetic shell that repels wet and wind from your upper and lower extremities. In intense cold your outer layer should be insulated for maximum warmth.

A cap, wool or synthetic, that covers your ears and the back of your neck is a necessity. A close-knit stocking cap works well. A soft pile cap with ear flaps and a drawstring to hold it closed around your head works great.

Lightweight gloves, wool or synthetic, are the preferred inner layer for hands. They will allow the performance of small tasks, such as opening your pack, without exposing your hands to the cold. Mittens, wool or synthetic, provide the insulation for your hands. Make sure your mittens fit over your gloves so you can dress your hands in layers as well. If you forgot your mittens, an extra pair of wool socks can be substituted in an emergency.

How to Wear Cold Weather Clothing

It is not the fact that you are wearing layers that protects you. You must ventilate the layers to allow the escape of moisture as you feel sweat being produced on your skin. You must peel off layers when ventilation no longer suffices. The layers, of course, are put back on when you feel a chill creeping in.

Better to start out from the car feeling slightly cold. You can "break a sweat" with a rush of perspiration, and you may soak your inner layers before you realize it. Say the trail begins to grow steeper, and you detect the wet warmth of sweat. Open an outer layer or two. The trail rises even more, so you take off an outer layer or two. At the top of the ridge you stop for a rest, and there you should replace a layer before all the heat you have produced has been lost. If you lose heat, your body will have to generate more heat. You are balancing body heat and sweat production with body heat and sweat loss in order to stay dry.

Wet Weather Clothing

By now you have probably come to appreciate the need to stay as dry as possible in wet weather. So you have chosen a wardrobe consisting of a lot of synthetic undergarments and midlayer garments, clothes that wick body moisture away from your skin and dry quickly with body heat if they get damp. Specifically for wet weather, you need upper and lower garments designed to keep you dry in extremes of wetness.

Synthetic shells are often advertised as being waterproof and breathable at the same time. Waterproof/breathable fabrics are produced by laminating an extremely thin film onto a more durable material. The film, with millions of microscopic pores, allows tiny sweat molecules to pass through while keeping larger water molecules, such as rain and snow, out. How well they work varies, depending on the ambient air temperature and moisture, and whether or not you have kept them relatively clean. Dirt can fill the pores and prevent them from functioning. You may find these garments comfortable on a day when it is cold and dry outside. You may find yourself wet with sweat inside one of these shells when a warm rain falls on a dirty parka.

Coated nylon shells are 100 percent waterproof, and they do not breathe. They allow no water to get in and no sweat to get out. You will not get wet from the rain, but you may create a sauna inside your coated raingear if you are exercising hard. In an environment known for heavy rains, though, choose coated nylon raingear.

For the upper half of your body, a parka with a roomy hood is the choice of most trekkers. For the bottom half of your body, the choice is most often rain pants. Full leg zippers make it easier to put on and take off pants and allow for better ventilation. Half-leg zippers are almost as easy to use.

From time to time, you may still see a trekker in the rain wearing a poncho. A poncho is essentially a small, waterproof tarp with a hooded hole in the middle for your head. Although ponchos can be spread out over your pack while you are hiking, they seldom please more than a rain parka and pair of pants do. If your pack is not waterproof—or at least water-resistant, you can buy a waterproof pack cover or carry a large garbage bag that will sort of fit over your pack.

Footwear

Does any part of the human anatomy talk more often, or more insistently, than a trekker's feet? And are they glad to be in the wild, unhurried outdoors? Nope. They complain! The question then arises: Can feet find true happiness squashed beneath a load into boots and socks on a wilderness trail?

Boots

As is most often true when selecting gear and clothing, you will find an array of befuddling choices in boots. Your choices fall, however, into one of three basic categories: lightweight, midweight, and heavyweight.

Lightweight "boots" look more like sport shoes, made for endeavors such as tennis or basketball. With uppers typically constructed of a fabric and a flexible sole, these boots are designed for short trips over easy to moderate terrain with a light load. You will, though, see trekkers deep in wild places with only lightweight boots.

Midweight boots usually have uppers similar to lightweights, but their overall construction is heavier and their sole construction is definitely heavier. They provide enough support for longer trips over moderate terrain with a heavier load.

Heavyweight boots, as the name implies, have strong rigid uppers and heavy soles of rugged material. The sole often contains a shank, a piece of slightly flexible or non-flexible material that runs two-thirds to the full length of the boot providing security on difficult terrain. Of course they are not as comfortable as lighter boots, but you gain safety and support for your feet and ankles on tricky ground while carrying a heavy load. Some heavyweight boots are made with plastic upper parts. You more often see them made with full-grain leather that uses the entire thickness of animal hide as opposed to split-grain leather. Since high grades of leather are relatively waterproof and breathable, most people end up preferring a leather boot. Better full-grain leather boots have the uppers stitched to the sole and an upper with few seams. Generally, the fewer the seams in the upper, the better the boot.

Choosing New Boots

The single most important factor in choosing a boot is the fit. When trying on boots, wear the socks you intend to hike in and lace up the boots. The second and third lacing fixtures down from the top of the boot are the ones that hold the heel in place. Be sure the laces are snug there. Your heel should, ideally, have no space for lateral movement, and a minimum of up and down movement—although new boots will always allow some up and down shifting of the heel.

At the ball of your foot, right at the base of your toes, there should be contact with the sides of the boot—a supportive pressure, not a cramped feeling. Along the arch of your foot you should feel gentle contact with the boot. From the ball forward there should be lessening contact, and your toes will be most content if they can wiggle freely.

Test the fit by pressing your booted foot firmly against a wall, checking to see if the contact points remain relatively constant, and if toes stay free. To check a fit do not kick the wall or grind out any deep knee bends, both of which are unrealistic and unenlightening.

To ease the complaints of poorly fitted feet, understand the critical importance of break-in time—the time required for your personal flex patterns to develop in new boots. For the first week wear the boots around the house or on short evening walks. By the end of the first week, you should be able to wear the boots all day, but keep wearing them around town for a second week before hitting the trail under a pack.

Socks

For maximum comfort and protection, wear two pairs of socks—a "sock system." The keys to a successful sock system are moisture transfer, motion between socks, and the ability to stand off the environment. Lightweight liner socks, wool or synthetic, provide a small amount of insulation but, more importantly, they create a "lubricating" layer than transfers friction away from your feet to help prevent blisters. They also transfer moisture from your feet into outer socks to help keep your feet dry. Wool or synthetic, heavyweight outer socks provide insulation and comfort. Trekkers should give special attention to padding in key areas, ball and heel, where impact is greatest. And, of course, the sock should fit.

General Principles in Choosing Clothing

▲ **Clothing should provide comfort and ease of movement.** Clothing should not restrict circulation. Loose-fitting clothing is typically the best choice. Some new stretch synthetics fit snug while providing the same comfort and ease of movement as loose-fitting clothing.

▲ **Clothing should provide insulation.** Clothing works as insulation by creating dead air spaces, air trapped between the fibers of the garment, that protect you from conductive and radiant heat loss. The best clothing does not lose its ability to insulate even when wet with water or sweat.

▲ **A windproof and waterproof outer shell** should be available at all times to protect you from convective and evaporative heat loss. Windproof does not always mean waterproof. Read the label.

▲ **Double-stitched seams, strong zippers, and reinforcement at areas of stress** (such as elbows, knees, and seats) are usually worth the money.

▲ **Functional designs** that include large pockets that fasten and unfasten easily, roomy hoods on parkas, leg zippers on wind and rain pants, and adjustable closures on wrists and ankles are usually worth the money.

> "The ability to simplify means to eliminate the unnecessary so that the necessary may speak."
> *Hans Hofman*

Going Light

In the modern backpacking era, there is nothing new about attempts to trim weight down to an absolute minimum. Once upon a time cutting the handles off toothbrushes, clipping the labels out of garments, and boring holes through anything you could reasonably bore a hole through to lighten the load was as commonplace as trail mix. What you can do today, however, is find gear and clothing that adds new meaning to the term "lightweight."

At *Backpacker,* editors, at least some of them, have made deep personal commitments to see how light they can go. Since none of them have died so far, disappeared, or given up backpacking, some of their suggestions are presented here:

Downsize. Remove products such as toothpaste and sunscreen from their original packaging and put them into film canisters. If your trek is long enough to require a resupply, include replacement canisters, already filled, in caches to reduce weight on your back. Consider a three-quarter-length sleeping pad instead of a full-length pad. Take a wilderness medicine course that includes a big dose of improvisation and cut down on the size of your medical kit. You can leave out medical supplies such as splinting materials and some specific wound management materials.

Double up. Boxer shorts can double as a swimsuit (but you might want to sew the fly shut). Stuff sacks can double as camp shoes when you wear them over socks. Sleeping in fleece pants and sweater can allow you to carry a lighter bag (but make sure you consider the room you will take up in the sleeping bag when you choose the size of your bag). Eat out of your cooking pot and leave the bowl behind.

Substitute. If you are willing to shop around (and sometimes spend quite a bit more money), you can find very lightweight tents, stoves, cookware, raingear, trail shoes, and other clothing. Lightweight shoes, for instance, can weigh more than two pounds less than leather boots. Point-and-shoot cameras weigh less than SLR cameras. Substitute halogen tablets for a water filter. With these substitutions, your lighter, less bulky stuff will fit into a smaller and therefore lighter pack.

Leave it out. Remove all packaging and leave it at home. Even granola bars, as an example, can be unwrapped and carried together in one plastic bag. Forget the camp chair. Plan meals that use one pot and leave the second one behind. Plan meals that cook fast, saving fuel. Plan meals carefully and leave extra food behind. And cut at least part of the handle off your toothbrush.

Nutrition and Food Preparation

Food is fuel. But that does not mean it has to taste like fuel. In fact, the longer the trek, the more you will want to plan meals that satisfy not only your needs but also your taste buds. Or, to put it another way, carry what you like to eat. It is true, however, that the nutritional value of food, its go-power, is worthy of consideration. A shortage of nutrients causes energy slumps that bring early fatigue, lassitude, mind-numbness, and a predisposition for getting sick or injured. A part of a wise start to every trek is a plan to eat nutritionally. Your body has three sources of energy: carbohydrates, fats, and, to some extent, proteins.

Carbohydrates (sugars and starches) digest the quickest and easiest. Simple carbohydrates (simple sugars: table sugar, brown sugar, date sugar, honey, molasses) break down very fast, entering the bloodstream soon after being chewed and swallowed. You get an energy boost right away. Most sugars burn so rapidly, however, your energy level can suddenly fall below your starting point if all you eat is simple carbohydrates. Complex carbohydrates (strings of simple sugars called starches) need to be a major portion of your trail diet. Starches break down more slowly, providing power for the long haul. As a general guideline, carbohydrates should supply around 60–70 percent of the calories of your trekking diet.

Fats are necessary—but not an awful lot of them. Fats break down slowly in the digestive process, so more time is required for them to become energy. That makes a fatty dinner a fine idea when you are anticipating a long, cold night in your bag. There are saturated fats and unsaturated fats, and most fats, animal and vegetable, are combinations of both. Saturated fats are harder, and stick to your arteries better, so they are considered less healthy than unsaturated fats. Fats tend to taste really good, which helps explain obesity, but they need only supply approximately 20–25 percent of your diet.

> ## Complete Protein Combinations
> 1. Combine rice with legumes, wheat, seeds, or dairy products.
> 2. Combine wheat with legumes, nuts, seeds, or dairy products.
> 3. Combine legumes with corn, seeds, whole grains, or dairy products.
> 4. Combine seeds with dairy products.
> 5. Combine potatoes with dairy products.

Proteins are made up of amino acids, and amino acids are the basic substance of human tissue. Proteins are not a primary energy source, but your body will use them if nothing else is available, or if you exercise for a long period of time. But, since tissue is continually lost and replaced (and new tissue is built when you exercise), proteins are essential to life. All of the amino acids are synthesized by your body, except for eight that have to be eaten. A "complete protein" has all eight of these amino acids. Eggs, dairy, and meat (including fish) are complete. Other foods, such as grains, seeds, nuts, and legumes contain incomplete proteins, but since they are incomplete in different ways, some of them can be combined to form complete proteins. Legumes (soybeans, navy beans, kidney beans, pinto beans, lima beans, peanuts, black-eyed peas, chickpeas, split peas, lentils) combine with seeds and nuts to form complete proteins, and dairy products and whole grains also combine completely. Most whole grains combine with most legumes to complete the protein package. Some dairy products combine with some seeds and nuts to form complete proteins. Proteins need to make up about 10–15 percent of your diet.

> ## Sources of Nutrition
> **Complex Carbohydrates:** whole grains and whole grain products (cereals, breads), pasta, fruits, vegetables
> **Fats:** butter, margarine, oils, cheeses, meats, nuts
> **Proteins:** meat, milk and dairy products, eggs, seeds, nuts, legumes, whole grains

Vitamins, Minerals, and Fiber

You will not function well or even for long without vitamins, and these little organic molecules must be eaten. They will not provide energy for the trail, but some do aid in the processing of food into energy. Thirteen vitamins are considered essential. Some are fat-soluble (A, D, E, K) and are stored in fatty tissue and organ tissue of the body. Some are water-soluble (C and the

B-complex of eight vitamins), cannot be stored, and wash out when you sweat or urinate. As long as you eat a balanced diet, you will probably get the vitamins you need. On extended treks, when balancing what you eat becomes problematic—at least some of the time—a daily multivitamin that meets the Recommended Daily Allowances (RDA) is not a bad idea. To exceed the RDA, especially with fat-soluble vitamins, may be harmful. The RDA of vitamins should be listed on the label.

Traces of several minerals are also required for you to continue to function. These minerals are generally divided into two classes: major minerals (such as calcium) that you need more of than minor minerals (such as iron). Once again, a balanced diet supplies all the minerals you need, and supplements should not exceed the RDA. Remember, taking vitamin/mineral supplements is sort of like cheating; they are not a substitute for eating right.

Fiber is stuff that exists in some foods that you eat, but it is stuff you do not digest. Still, it plays a vital role in health. There are two kinds of fibers: insoluble (whole grain products, bran, cellulose) and soluble (oats, oat bran, fruits, vegetables, nuts, beans). Insoluble fiber will not hold much water, so it moves quickly through your digestive tract, and encourages other food to move quickly, keeping your bowel movements regular. Too much insoluble fiber may produce too much movement. Soluble fiber, on the other side of the nutritional coin, absorbs water and becomes gooey, sticking to other foods and slowing their assimilation into your body. This is healthy because soluble fibers stick to some potentially harmful cholesterol better than your body does—and carries it out into the cat hole.

Nutrition in the Cold Outdoors

Although your need for vitamins and minerals does not change, your need for water and your energy requirements increase as the temperature decreases. To meet the increased need, you should drink more and eat more. The nutrient breakdown should be approximately 60 percent carbohydrate, 25 percent fat, and 15 percent protein. Carbohydrate intake is especially important to replenish muscle energy stores in order to prevent excess fatigue that often leads to cold injury (see "Health and Safety" in On the Trail). Cold tolerance may be improved for most people by a high-fat snack (about one-third the calories from fat) every couple of hours: one or two snacks between breakfast and lunch, another one between lunch and dinner, and one more before crawling into your sleeping bag. If you are one of those people who awake cold during the night, pack a snack into your sleeping bag.

> **Success Tip**
>
> Fill a water bottle with hot chocolate before bedtime. In the sleeping bag, it provides warmth by contact. Later in the night, it provides warmth by calories.

Nutrition at High Altitude

Higher altitudes tend to be cold, and the same cold-weather recommendations apply, with one exception, fat is not tolerated as well at higher altitudes—approximately 16,000 feet and above. Fat tolerance decreases as altitude increases. You will probably function better if you change high-fat snacks to high-energy, high-carbohydrate snacks. There is also some evidence indicating that people on high-carb diets—about 70 percent carbohydrate—acclimatize better to higher altitudes. Because altitude often affects your appetite, it is critical to carry food you crave. Proper nutrition is important, but not as important as an adequate caloric and fluid intake.

The Food Bag

Packing a few fresh foods to be downed early in the trek is not a bad idea, but most of your specific food choices need to take survivability of the food into account. How disappointing, and perhaps devastating, to dig into your food bag and discover good grub gone bad. Too much heat and rough handling in an overstuffed pack can produce green fuzz on breadstuff and cheese, reduce crackers to crumbs, and transform a stick of salami into a ticking time bomb of bacteriological destruction. But I have packed for as long as 62 days, including resupplies, and had none of the palatables become unpalatable.

General suggestions for keeping food good:

▲ Choose dry foods that keep a long time.
▲ Avoid fatty meats and dairy products since they spoil quickly, but you can pack a few cans of meat if you are willing to pack out the empty cans.
▲ Carry a resealable plastic container and plastic mug instead of a bowl and cup, and pack fragile foods such as cookies and crackers in them.
▲ Keep air and moisture, the support team for bacterial growth, out of food repackaged in plastic bags.
▲ Protect food from heat, which fosters bacterial growth. Pack perishables deep in your pack to insulate them, and chill them in cold water or snow whenever possible.

Specifically speaking:

Breads. Carry tortillas, bagels, pita, and rye bread. These breads will deform from compression over time, but they remain okay to eat for the longest amount of time. Flour tortillas stay mold-free the longest of all. Leave behind fresh baked breadstuff such as white and wheat bread, muffins, and baguettes.

Cereals. Long a trekking staple, dry cereals endure extremely well. Instant cereals—oatmeal, cream of wheat—can be repackaged from their individual packages into a larger plastic bag if you cannot find them in bulk. Granolas will, however, lose their crunch in the heat and after repeated exposure to air.

> ## Sulphured vs. Unsulphured
>
> Many dried fruits (read the label) have a form of sulphur, usually sulphur dioxide, added as a preservative. This is especially true of light-colored fruits such as apples, apricots, peaches, and pears. Sulphur keeps the appealing fruit color from turning into an unappealing brown while doing nothing, almost everyone agrees, to alter the taste. Sulphur does improve longevity in fruit, but it does not promote human health—although it does not seem to hurt except in individuals who are sulphur-sensitive.

Cheeses. The lower the fat content, the longer the cheese will last. Processed cheeses, despite the loss of gustatorial delight, will last longest since a lot of microorganisms are processed out. Cheeses in individually sealed packages will last the longest of all, but create more waste to pack out. In most cases, green mold on cheese can be cut away (and packed out) leaving the rest of the hunk okay to consume.

Pasta. Inexpensive, easy to prepare, long-lasting, and available in a variety of shapes and flavors, pasta remains an excellent choice for the long trail.

Rice. Durable to the max, rice ranks high among foods you should pack. Instant rice has lost some of its nutritional value, but its quick-fix quality makes it worthy of consideration.

Assorted other grains. Couscous, bulgur, and falafel have great trail stamina, and provide variety when you are planning a lot of meals.

Potatoes. In the flake, pearl, or dehydrated hash brown form, potatoes are simply excellent and virtually immune to spoilage. Flakes and pearls prepare instantly with the addition of hot water. Hash browns take a bit of work, but they are worth it for delicious variety at breakfast or dinner.

Meats. The drier the meat the longer it lasts. Jerky of all kinds will last an incredibly long time. Pepperoni sticks hold up well and better than sliced pepperoni. Most other meats should be avoided.

Crackers. Some crackers get more than half their calories from fat and contain several times the daily recommended intake of salt. On the other hand, fat free, low-sodium crackers may provide a healthy dose of fiber and a nice hunk of nutrition if the "whole wheat" on the front of the package is true. Bottom line: Read the ingredients. Low fat crackers will remain safely edible for a long time, despite their tendency to turn into dust in your pack. But even the dust is tasty, especially sprinkled over a dish of something else.

Nuts and seeds. All nuts and seeds have excellent trail stamina. And they mix well with other foods as additions to cereals or sprinkles on top of dinners.

Candy. Bacteria will not grow on sugar. Candy, in other words, will last. But candy susceptible to melting, especially chocolate, can become an unrecognizable mess in heat. Yogurt-covered snacks are best left behind.

Energy bars. Expensive, but they last a very long time, and they do provide a whopping dose of energy for the weight.

Cookies. Large and soft ones crumble much faster than smaller, drier cookies, and fruit bars mush into a solid mass—but they all remain edible for a long time.

Fruits. Sun-drying remains popular, but many fruits today are dehydrated with forced hot air. Either way the water in the fruit evaporates, changing from about 80 percent to as low as 15 percent. Most of the vitamin C evaporates, too, leaving condensed minerals and fiber, and a hunk of sugar—the sugar content of many dried fruits is higher than most cookies and some candies. Neither way, sun or forced hot air, creates a better food, but both ways create a very long-lasting trail food.

> "If a man has nothing to eat, fasting is the most intelligent thing he can do."
> *Hermann Hesse*

Ration and Menu Planning

Manufacturers of freeze-dried fare have reached great heights in the science of food storage, adding life not only to how long food will last but also to nutrition, taste, and texture. I have consumed and evaluated literally hundreds of packages of camp food for *Backpacker,* and I will carry many of those meals again and again. You can plan an entire trek, foodwise, by reading the labels on freeze-dried and dehydrated meals and buying what you need to fuel your journey. It costs more. It

Freeze-dried vs. Dehydrated

Freeze-dried food has undergone a unique process that goes something like this: The food, cooked or fresh, is frozen very solid then placed in freezing temperatures with warm air flowing around it long enough for the moisture to sublimate off. Since ice crystals never form, the cells of the food remain relatively undamaged and most of the nutrition is left intact. More than 99 percent of the food's water content is removed, so the result is very light in weight, and the bulk is reduced a little. And since the cells are undamaged, they hydrate quickly and easily.

Dehydrated food, a similar product, is exposed to low heat in order to drive the water out. Old dehydration methods drove out a lot of nutrition as well. Current methods preserve much of the nutritional value. A dehydrated product has 90–97 percent of its water removed. Dehydration shrinks the size of the cells, reducing a lot of the weight and bulk, and increasing the time it takes to hydrate the food.

The quality of the hydrated food, whether freeze-dried or dehydrated, depends primarily on the quality of the food before the water was removed. Buy from a recognized manufacturer and the quality is assured. Many companies now offer their foods in resealable bags that allow rehydration to take place worry free within the package.

leaves you with more trash. It is simple, and it works. And if that is your choice, you can skip the rest of this section. But on a long trek, even if you choose to cook from "scratch," a few add-water-and-eat meals in the bottom of the food bag will give you the option of a fast, hot dinner when you do not want to cook—not a bad idea. If you would rather approach most of your cooking and eating in a more creative, and admittedly time-consuming, way, then read on.

A Ration Plan

Basically you have two options beyond freeze-dried: ration planning and menu planning. A ration plan works for solo hikers up to groups of any size. It grants you the freedom to pack a wide variety of dried foods that allow for an almost endless variety of meal options. You plan each meal as you go. You are allowed spontaneity, adapting to the day's preferences and tasks. Since you are cooking from "scratch," you minimize pre-packaged foods, and thus cost and trash.

The ration plan presented here is based on years of experimentation. The weights and caloric values are estimates, but they have proven to provide the energy necessary for the long trail. If you would rather plan more precisely, a chart of caloric values for some popular foods along with their weights can be found below.

Here is the basic ration plan: Figure the numbers of days you will be on the trail, and the number of people who will be eating, and carry the necessary weight of a variety of foods to match the days and the number of people.

An example: If two people are planning a 10-day trek in the Colorado Rockies in July, they can pack 1.75 pounds of food per person per day. Two times 10 gives you 20 days of eating. Twenty times 1.75 gives you 35 pounds of food, or 17.5 pounds per person for the trek.

The Necessary Weight in Food

▲ In very warm conditions, when your activity level is very low, you can pack 1.5 pounds of food per person per day. The calories will add up to approximately 2200–2500 per person per day if you carry the recommended types of food listed below. Examples of this type of trek are water-based trips where you supplement your diet with fishing and/or some fresh and canned food.

▲ From spring through fall, with the typical exertion required for the usual trekking conditions, you can pack 1.75–2 pounds of food per person per day. The calories will add up to roughly 2500–3000 per person per day.

▲ In cold environments or when the trek will require an unusual amount of physical effort, pack 2–2.25 pounds of food per person per day. The calories will add up to roughly 3000–3500 per day.

▲ In the most extreme environments—extreme cold, high altitude mountaineering, Continental Divide thru-hikers—pack 2.5 pounds of food per person per day or more. At this level eating becomes a discipline more than a result of hunger.

Calories/Pound of Specific Foods

	Calories/Pound			Calories/Pound
Breakfast			Bagels	1800
Cream of wheat	1658		Cashews	2604
Granola	2211		Chocolate bars	1650
Hash browns (dried)	1600		Crackers	1828
Oatmeal	1672		Coconut	2468
			Dates	1243
Dinners			Fruit bars	3000
Bulgur	1621		Hard candy	1751
Couscous	1600		Mixed nuts	2694
Egg noodles	1760		Pita bread	1000
Falafel	2200		Peanuts	2558
Lentils	1860		Popcorn	1642
Macaroni	1674		Raisins	1360
Potatoes (sliced)	1624		Sunflower seeds	2550
Potato flakes	1650		Trail mix	2000
Refried beans	2200		Walnuts	2950
Rice	1647			
Spaghetti	1674		**Drinks and Sugar**	
Tortillas	1200		Brown sugar	1700
			Fruit crystals	1950
High Fat (High Calorie) Items			Honey	1379
Cheddar	1840		Hot chocolate	2000
Cream cheese	1600		White sugar	1700
Mozzarella (whole milk)	1280			
Parmesan	2080		**Desserts**	
Swiss	1680		Cheesecake	3500
Sour cream	1600		Pudding	1637
Margarine	3200			
Oil	4000		**Miscellaneous**	
Bacon pieces	2836		Chicken base	1117
Ham	1800		Beef base	1082
Peanut butter	2682		Corn (dried)	1600
Pepperoni	2255		Instant soups (1 cup)	100
Salami	2041		Eggs (powdered)	2697
Smoked salmon	800		Milk (dried, nonfat)	1625
Tuna (water packed)	720		Peas and carrots (dried)	1200
Tuna (oil packed)	880		Peas and onions (dried)	1200
			Peppers (dried)	1000
Trail Food			Ramen noodles	1067
Apples	1102		Soup mix (veggie)	1600
Apricots	1080		Tomato base	1350

Types of Food

Ration planning is not an exact science. There is a lot of flexibility with the types of foods, but it is important your total weight measures up. If you come up light when you weigh your food bag, throw in a couple of your favorite items. If you come up heavy, get rid of something.

▲ **Breakfast.** Bagels, cream of wheat, oatmeal, granola, hash browns. Make these foods equal approximately 15 percent of the total weight.

▲ **Dinner.** Bulgur, couscous, dried potatoes, falafel, lentils, pasta, instant beans, rice, tortillas. Make these foods about 30 percent of the total weight.

▲ **High fat additions.** Cheese, margarine, meats, oil, peanut butter. Make these foods equal about 15 percent of the total weight.

▲ **Trail food.** Candy, crackers, dried fruit, fruit bars, energy bars, pita bread, nuts and seeds, trail mix. Make these foods about 20 percent of the total weight.

▲ **Drinks and sugars.** Drink mixes, honey, hot chocolate, sugar. Make these foods about 10 percent of the total weight.

▲ **Desserts.** Quick cheesecakes, instant pudding, cookies. Make these foods about 5 percent of the total weight.

▲ **Miscellaneous.** Instant milk, dried soups, powdered eggs. Make these foods about 5 percent of the total weight.

A Menu Plan

To save the time and effort of thinking—sometimes an important consideration after a long day on the trail—you can menu plan instead of ration plan. With a menu plan, you need to figure out the exact numbers of each meal you will need: How many breakfasts, lunches, and dinners? Then decide what each meal will consist of. Then pack everything you need for that meal into one plastic bag. For example, at dinnertime you pull out a dinner bag containing just the right amount of rice, dried beans, cheese, drink mix, and cookies for one dinner for the number

Spice Up Your Life

A spice kit can be the best of friends at mealtime, even when you go freeze-dried. You can turn the unsavory into the savory, and the bland into a blessing. You can also ruin dinner, so remember to add spices a little at a time. Some spices, the peppers for instance, increase in strength as they cook, so wait a while between dashes and taste-tests. In a group, spices can be added to individual portions to satisfy particular sets of buds. Popular spices include:

▲ Salt
▲ Basil
▲ Black pepper
▲ Cayenne pepper
▲ Cinnamon

▲ Cumin powder
▲ Curry powder
▲ Garlic powder
▲ Onion flakes
▲ Parsley flakes

If You Hate to Cook

If cooking just turns you off, there are options other than the usual freeze-dried smorgasbord of products.

1. **Meals, Ready-to-Eat (MRE).** Thank the U.S. military. In a full field package MRE you will find entrée, bread, dessert, snack, juice, coffee, gum, even a spoon and napkin, all packaged in indestructible plastic bags. You might see similar products, at least the entrées, on supermarket shelves being sold as "retort" foods— foods that have been cooked and sealed in a flexible foil package that you just throw in hot water to reheat, sort of like a soft can. MREs show up semiregularly in army-navy surplus stores, on the Internet, and, sometimes, in outdoor specialty stores. If you are willing to shell out a little more money, you can purchase MREs packaged with a unique warming element. The retort goes in a plastic bag with the element to which a dash of water is added to stimulate an amazing amount of heat. Result: a hot and very tasty breakfast, lunch, or dinner—with zero cooking. Some manufacturers of famous backpacking foods are now offering a similar product. Pros: Long-life, no clean up. Cons: More weight, more cost, and a lot more trash.

2. **Grocery store and go.** You can walk out of your favorite food market with instant cereals such as oatmeal and cream of wheat. Throw in some butter, nuts, and/or dried fruit to extend the staying power of cereals. Tea, instant coffee, sugar, and powdered milk for hot drinks are easy to carry. Instant soups are available by the ton, including the perennial favorite ramen noodles. With tortillas, instant beans, cheese, and salsa you can whip up a warm dinner in the time it takes to raise water to the boiling point. Or pick up a few varieties of dinner-in-a-bag. They take about ten minutes of boiling, and the manufacturers suggest adding milk (powdered works fine) and butter or margarine. Pros: Inexpensive, easy, lightweight. Cons: Pots and cups to wash.

3. **Cold camping.** No fire. No stove. No mess. No bother. No hot food. The elements of cold camping. Break your fast with bagels and cream cheese, or granola and powdered milk. Add some dried fruit for flavor and a nutritional boost. Lunch on GORP, fruit bars, energy bars, fresh fruit, meat sticks, cheese, crackers, pita bread, or more bagels. Dine on the same. Drink water, or throw in some fruit drink crystals or a powdered energy drink for variety and a few more calories. Pros: Inexpensive, easy. Cons: More weight.

of people who will be eating. As a final check, weigh all the meal bags together after packing them to make sure you have approximately the right amount of weight to meet your caloric needs.

Resupplies

Week after week, for more than seven weeks in Idaho, I returned again and again to a central cache that hung suspended between two trees, about 10 feet off the ground, well out of reach of bears and at least troublesome to access for little

A stove can do everything you need for meal preparation without harming the environment (NOLS/Deborah Sussex).

critters: The cache had been flown in. In Wyoming, I had a prearranged rendezvous with a horsepacker. In Argentina, the resupply came in on mule back. In Utah, I hiked in a couple of times from an access road that vaguely paralleled my route, and buried caches in the sand of a long serpentine canyon.

A resupply gives you the chance to refill your fuel bottle as well as your food bag. Sometimes I have sent myself clean clothes. If you meet the resupplier, you can send out trash and mail. If, and only if, you will be coming back later to pick it up, you can stow trash at a cache when you resupply. But all of my resupplies have had one thing in common: The sense of celebration accompanying new food and the discovery of small surprises—a bag of candy, a book—that I included.

Somewhere between a week and 10 days worth of food is all you will want your back to carry. And gear is not exempt from the principle of resupply. You might want an ice axe and crampons for a section of your trek—so you cache them at the beginning of that section, pick them up, and cache them at the end of that section (to be taken home later). Where you are trekking, of course, determines where and how you will be resupplied—but here are a few things to consider:

▲ You can mail a resupply to yourself via general delivery if your route passes near a post office.

▲ You can have a friend meet you at a prearranged trailhead. A nice touch here is fresh food and a bottle of wine, both of which may be consumed before you hit the trail again.

▲ You can stash a cache in a vehicle, and park it at a trailhead along your route.

▲ You can sometimes arrange for a horsepacker to resupply you. Keep in mind that horses cannot reach all the places you can, and the packer may turn down your first choice of rendezvous sites. The cost of a resupply starts to rise dramatically when a horse is involved.

▲ You can sometimes arrange a resupply by air. Variables here include the legality and practicality of an aircraft landing, especially a fixed-wing aircraft. Helicopters offer more freedom in landing zones. The cost of a helicopter may be three to four times the cost of a small fixed-wing plane, and both price tags may be prohibitive.

▲ You can hike in ahead of time, when access routes exist, and drop your own caches.

Stove Fuels and Stoves

Fuels. Before choosing the stove, you need to choose the fuel. To me there are only three fuels worth considering: kerosene, butane, and white gas. And kerosene does not deserve too much thought from most people. Kerosene is cheap, but it stinks, burns without producing as much heat as the other two fuels, and tends to coat everything with a greasy film.

Butane comes contained in cartridges that pack neatly, light quickly without priming, and burn cleanly. The cartridges themselves, of course, add weight on your back. Butane does not burn as hot as white gas, but it usually does the job. One instance when it might fail you is when the temperature is low. The lower the temperature the less efficiently butane works. It can freeze up in the cartridge on a really cold day. A solution is to sleep with it in your sleeping bag. But sleeping with it does not solve another problem: Fuel in a cartridge does not let you see how much is left. Without another cartridge waiting in your pack, you may live in fear the next meal may be your last hot one. Or perhaps worse, you get a meal half cooked and the stove sputters to a devastating halt.

Thus white gas, carried in a separate container from which you fill the stove every day, usually serves best. You always know how much fuel you have, and after a few trials, you can estimate very closely how much you will need for a trip. It burns very hot, clean, and virtually odorless no matter how low the temperature sinks. If you want an easy fire some night, white gas can be used as a firestarter—if you do not mind being called less than extraordinary as an outdoorsperson. Overall, you carry less weight with white gas. You can buy white gas around the world.

Liquid fuel needs vary with the length of the trip and the season of the year (NOLS/Tom Bol).

Does white gas have problems? Yep. For one thing it requires priming. Well-made backcountry stoves come with a built-in priming mechanism that almost always works. Squeeze tubes of primer can be purchased for emergencies. If a hot stove blows out in a stiff wind, it is often difficult to restart until it has cooled. White gas stoves require pumping to put the fuel under enough pressure to rise to the burner. When your hands are cold you can come to hate that.

Another potential problem is the extreme explosiveness of white gas. Extra white gas needs to be stored away from flames, and stoves need to be kept clean and checked often for leaks. If a jet of burning gas erupts from an inappropriate orifice in your stove, run away until it burns itself out.

Stoves. When you know what fuel you will burn, you can choose a stove. But which stove? Here are some things to consider:

▲ Since the stove may rest on uneven surfaces, choose one with wide enough supports to provide a stable base.

▲ Since you do not want to always cook—and cannot cook some meals—over a blast furnace, choose a stove that simmers.

▲ Since you do not want to spend a lot of time firing up your stove, choose one that lights easily.

▲ Since you are concerned about weight, consider the ounces the stove adds to your pack.

▲ Since you will be depending on your stove a long time, and since even the best ones might break down, choose a stove you can repair in the field (and be sure to carry the appropriate stove repair kit).

▲ Since the wind will blow, choose a stove with a windscreen or buy one separately.

▲ If you will be cooking on snow, carry a flat metal plate, such as a license plate, to support the stove. Or use the blade of a snow shovel.

Fire Cooking

Back when it was ethically acceptable, I went out for a month or more, several times, with no stove. Cooking on an open fire, rapidly becoming a lost art, can add a heaping measure of fun, wonder, and dietary ash to your next trek. Providing, of course, campfires are legal where you are camped, and you follow the guidelines of Leave No Trace (see "Leave No Trace" in On the Trail). This is not a treatise on fire cooking—it is, more than anything else, some thoughts to consider in case your stove totally poops out.

You will want to make sure the forest deck provides adequate fuel of just the right size from twiggies to downed and dead branches no thicker around than your wrist. Time remains decidedly a major element in preparing food over the burning remnants of what was once a tree. A campfire cook is no better than the fire he or

You can cook on fires when they are ethically acceptable and as environmentally friendly as possible (NOLS/Deborah Sussex).

she builds. Keep it small and keep the heat concentrated. Most meals indeed will be cooked over coals since flames create far too much heat unless you are a fan of the mountain-man's-raw-meat-seared-black-on-the-outside or more modern noodles-baked-to-the-consistency-of-cement on the floor of the pot. And, to prevent adding injury to insult, a roaring blaze makes it mighty hard on the chef. The fire, on most days, really needs to be no larger than the bottom of the frying pan or pot you will cook in.

Gather enough firewood to prevent a trip for more in the middle of preparation of the food. Once the tinder is burning well, add larger pieces but not so large they will take forever to burn down to coals. When the coals are a couple of inches thick, you are ready to cook. If you are intent on a larger fire, scrape coals off to the side of the flame, far enough from the main fire to prevent its heat from affecting meal preparation.

You can set your pot directly in the coals, but you can regulate the heat better if you build a support—with rocks of varying sizes—for the pot above the heat. The bigger the rock, the farther from the heat your pot sits. And do not plan on stepping away from the kitchen for more than a moment or two. An unwatched pot not only boils, it quickly turns dinner into a scorched ruin over wood heat.

Cookware

On the simple side of things, you can get by with a pot in which to boil water. But the simple side is also the uninteresting side—and the longer the trek the more interested you will be in preparing interesting meals. You will want lightweight, durable, and functionally simple cookware. You will have, again, many choices. The cost, the material, and perhaps the special features, will all become a part of your decision.

Cookware Materials

Aluminum. Lightest and cheapest, aluminum is the material of choice for most trekkers—but be sure it has a nonstick coating to prevent scorching and to ease cleaning.

Stainless steel. Rugged enough to handle serious bumps and bruises, stainless steel pots are a good choice for trekkers who want their gear to last a long while. The main downside is that steel pots weigh considerably more than aluminum.

Titanium. For ounce-counting hikers with a bit of cash to spare, featherweight titanium pots cannot be beat. But plan on keeping a close eye on dinner since heat transference is fast and furious.

Composite. Some manufacturers fuse aluminum and stainless steel together to take advantage of their respective advantage: steel on the inside to reduce scorching and aluminum on the outside to save weight. Expect a higher price tag for composite pots.

Thoughts on Pot and Pan Picking

The number and capacity of the pots and pans you pack should correspond to the number of hikers in your party and to the complexity of your ration or menu plan. Usually listed in liters, a 1-liter capacity pot will hold slightly less than a quart. Pans are typically listed in inches describing their width. Here are some other thoughts to consider:

1-liter pot. Will boil a few cups of water for hot drinks or two small servings of pasta. Also works well as a saucepan for larger groups. Small canister stoves will nest inside a 1-liter pot.

1.5-liter pot. Large enough to hold one-pot meals for an average couple or for side dishes in a bigger party. Most backpacking stoves will nest inside this pot.

The choices in pots and pans are virtually unlimited (NOLS).

2-liter pot. Room for enough water to make hot drinks for six, or one dinner entrée for three hungry hikers.

3-liter pot. Seldom needed unless you are planning on cooking for a party of six or more.

Number of pots. Hot-water-only cooks can get by fine with one pot. If you have a ration or menu plan you will want at least two, one for cooking and one for mixing ingredients.

Pans. A frying pan adds delightful opportunities for cooking. A 10-inch pan will do in most cases, but a smaller one will suffice for two people who envision no great endeavors over the stove. A pan with a snug-fitting lid allows for baking.

Cookware Features

▲ **Lids.** Water boils faster, thus saving fuel, if your pots have a snug-fitting lid. Many manufacturers offer sets of pots that use the same lid. A frying pan can often substitute as a lid for a pot.

▲ **Bail handle.** Like the handle on a bucket, these wire loops let you grab and carry big pots with ease. Caution is required, though, because these handles get hot when they rest against the side of a hot pot.

A Basic Kitchen Kit

1. Personal cup, bowl, and spoon
2. Multipurpose tool (including knife, can opener, and pliers for potgrips)
3. Pot(s) with lid(s)
4. Frying pan with lid
5. Small spatula for frying
6. Water bottle with measurements marked on side
7. Kitchen cleaning kit (scrubber and soap)

- ▲ **Swing handle.** These handles swing out from the side of a pot or flip out from inside a frying pan. Even though they can get hot, you can use them instead of carrying potgrips.
- ▲ **Potgrip.** This little device is a necessity for picking up hot pots in most camp kitchens. A multipurpose tool can be used as a potgrip.
- ▲ **Lipped rim.** A rim that curves gently to the outside makes a pot easier to grab with potgrips and less prone to bending and warping under pressure.
- ▲ **Exterior finish.** For maximum heat absorption and faster boiling times, look for pots coated with a dark color. One night of cooking over the open flames of a campfire will readily blacken a shiny pot, but this type of blackening spreads throughout your pack.
- ▲ **Interior nonstick finish.** A must for aluminum pots and a welcome addition to any camp cookware, a nonstick finish limits scorching and burned-on messes. Cleanup is made easier.
- ▲ **Rounded bottom edges.** This feature encourages even heat distribution up the walls of the pot and eliminates hard-to-clean messes in the corners.
- ▲ **Nesting pots.** If your pot set does not allow the pots to fit neatly inside each other, choose another pot set.
- ▲ **Stuff sack.** If your cook set comes with one, carry it and use it. Blackened pots keep their black off your other stuff. If your stove fits inside your pots, you have everything conveniently bundled.

> "The world is impermanent.
> One should constantly remember death."
> *Sri Ramakrishna*

Health and Safety

"An ounce of prevention is worth a pound of cure," and so, with that in mind, here are a few recommendations to be considered prior to ever exposing yourself to the injuries and illnesses of the long trail.

1. If you have not had a physical or dental checkup recently, consider getting both before heading out. You make sure your gear and clothing are ready—make sure your body is ready, too. How soon is "recently"? Most physicians recommend an annual checkup, and the older you get the more important the annual checkup becomes. Dentists suggest an exam every six months.

2. Read the portion of this book dedicated to "Health and Safety" in the section On the Trail. Many of the recommendations are preventative, and suggestions concerning what medical supplies to carry are included there.

3. If you have never been trained in wilderness medicine, or if your skills are "out of shape," consider a course. Sources of training are listed in Appendix A.

First-aid Kits

Things to keep in mind:

▲ There is no such thing as the perfect trekking first-aid kit. Many factors will come into play when you choose the specific contents of your kit: your medical expertise, the environmental extremes you will face (such as high altitude), the number of people the kit will serve, the number of days the kit will be in use, the distance you will be from definitive medical care, and preexisting problems, such as diabetes, of group members.

▲ To save weight and space, choose specific items for the kit, whenever possible, that are versatile rather than particular. For example, medical adhesive tape has limited usefulness compared to duct tape.

A Suggested First-aid Kit
1. Adhesive bandage strips
2. Sterile gauze pads and/or sterile gauze rolls
3. Athletic tape, one inch by ten yards, and/or duct tape
4. Tincture of benzoin compound
5. Wound closure strips
6. Microthin film dressings
7. Moleskin and/or molefoam
8. Gel wound coverings
9. Soap-impregnated cleaning sponges
10. Elastic wrap
11. Rubber gloves
12. Sharp-tipped tweezers
13. Irrigation syringe
14. Safety pins
15. Pocket rescue mask

▲ Be familiar with the proper uses of all the items in the your kit before you need to use them.

▲ Evaluate and repack your kit before every trip. Renew medications that have reached expiration dates. Replace items that have been damaged by heat, cold, or moisture.

▲ Encourage each group member to pack and carry a personal first-aid kit in order to reduce the size and weight of the general kit.

Drugs to the Rescue

With adequate training, you will be able to improvise many of the items you might want—such as splinting materials—in order to deal with an emergency on the trail. Not so with medications. Although some "natural" remedies could be available growing near at foot, use of them requires specific knowledge you might not have. And few, if any, of them will work as fast or as aggressively as you might need.

Success Tip
Always know and carry in writing, preferably from your doctor, specific directions concerning how and when to use drugs you choose or need to pack.

Thoughts on Specific Nonprescription Drugs

Acetaminophen. For relief of pain of headache, cold and flu discomfort, minor muscle and joint discomfort, and menstrual cramps. Reduces fever. Especially useful for those who are allergic to aspirin or aspirin-containing products. Does not work well as an anti-inflammatory.

Antacid tablets. For symptomatic relief of heartburn, acid indigestion, sour stomach, and other conditions related to an upset stomach.

Antibiotic ointment. Contains ingredients that may help prevent infection in minor wounds, encourages healing of wounds, works as a lubricant, provides minor relief for itching.

Antihistamine. For the temporary relief of respiratory allergy symptoms and cold symptoms. Helps relieve the itching of allergic skin reactions. May be used as a mild sedative.

Aspirin. Same uses as acetaminophen but does work as an anti-inflammatory. Not to be given to children. Many people are allergic to aspirin.

Decongestant spray. For relief of nasal congestion that accompanies cold and allergies. May be useful to help stop nosebleed.

Decongestant tablets. For symptomatic relief of sinus headache pain and pressure caused by sinus congestion. A multipurpose cold medicine.

Diarrhea medication. For use, of course, in the control of diarrhea.

Ibuprofen. For symptomatic relief of pain associated with headache, colds, flu, frostbite, toothache, arthritis, burns, and menstrual cramps. For pain of inflammation associated with muscle and joint injury and overuse. Helps reduce fever.

Thoughts on Specific Prescription Drugs

Since prescription drugs require consultation with a doctor in order to acquire them, you must also acquire specific directions about how and when to use them.

Analgesics (painkillers). Serious pain will not be touched by over-the-counter painkillers. Ask you doctor about narcotics.

Antibiotics. Nasty infections of body parts such as skin, bones, the respiratory system, the urinary tract, and the gastrointestinal tract can be disabling and sometimes deadly, and antibiotics may be needed to kill the invading pathogens.

Allergy medication. A life-threatening allergic reaction (anaphylaxis) can only be reversed with injectable epinephrine.

Altitude medication. Drugs, such as acetazolamide and dexamethasone, prevent and treat illnesses associated with high altitude.

Diarrhea medication. Serious—and sometimes life-threatening—diarrhea often requires a prescription-strength drug.

Men and women often face different concerns on the trail (NOLS/Tom Bol).

For Women Only

by Annette McGivney, Southwest editor for Backpacker

Women can have as much fun trekking as the next guy. But women and men are not created equal—at least not when it comes to certain anatomy-specific health concerns.

Altitude and pregnancy. Should mom-to-be and baby-in-the-womb be subjected to high altitude hikes? Since the subject has not been researched much, a definitive answer is elusive. There was, however, one study that found it was safe for healthy women with a normal pregnancy to go from sea level to 8200 feet. For women who live at altitude, it is probably safe to assume they could hike a little higher, maybe to 10,000 feet, without complications. But go any higher and there is a chance the fetus could begin to suffer from lack of oxygen. And, according to Peter Hackett, M.D., a world-renowned high altitude medical expert, an additional reason for pregnant women to avoid high mountain elevations has to do "with remoteness from medical care should a problem arise. If you really want a healthy baby, why take such a risk?" Bottom line: Do not camp higher than 8200 feet if you live at sea level, or higher than 10,000 feet if you live at 5000 feet or more.

Your odds of avoiding complications at elevation will improve if you are physically fit and spend 2–4 days acclimatizing to moderate altitudes (5000–8000 feet) before going higher. Also watch for the signs and symptoms of altitude sickness: headache, nausea, trouble sleeping, unusual fatigue, shortness of breath, stumbling or "drunken" behavior (see "Health and Safety" in On the Trail). Pregnant women who experience premature contractions should stop all physical activity and be evacuated by litter or helicopter to a medical facility.

Nursing and trekking. After enduring the physical activity restrictions of the final trimester of pregnancy, many new moms are eager to hit the trail once baby is born. But what if you are nursing? The easiest option, by far, is for nursing moms to bring baby along. If the trip you desire is not suitable for baby, it is possible to "pump and dump" but it is still hard to keep from becoming engorged—an extremely painful condition when hiking. If you choose this option, use a small battery operated pump instead of a manual one to extract as much milk as possible. (Milk should be sumped in a hole like gray water.) Use the pump at home for a few days before the trip to make sure you can maintain the flow without complications. Also, do not pump double the normal amount in the days before your trip to provide for baby when you are gone. This will only increase your flow on the trail and make it more likely that you will become engorged. Better to pump an extra bottle a day over a period of a month and freeze it, or supplement with formula.

> "How old would you be if you didn't know how old you was?"
> *Satchel Paige*

Trekking with Children

Question: What keeps kids off treks?
Answer: Parents.

True, some kids are not ready for extended journeys beyond hard walls and soft carpets, but more often mom and dad are not ready. Children on treks do take more forethought, more preparation, and more care on the trail. There was a time, not really that long ago, when my son made up most of the load on one trekker's back, and somebody else bore the weight of his clothing, and the weight of the kid-packer's stuff. But I can tell you this with certainty: It was worth it. I remember, for instance, a chill rain drenching everything in a camp in the High Uintas of Utah except his spirit. Long live the child—and the child still in each of us.

But kids are not little adults. They run differently, and they break down differently. That is why there is a branch of medicine called "pediatrics," a word derived from the Greek word for "child-treatment."

Kids and food. I know what my kids will eat, and you know what your kids will eat, and those are edibles that should be in our food bag. Save experimenting with new foods for home. Sometimes kids do not realize they are hungry and thirsty, so offer water and nutritious snacks often. The long trail demands a lot of energy, so carry more food than you think you will need.

Kids and heat. Children gain core heat faster than adults. Little human cooling systems work fine, mostly, but they sometimes need encouragement. The younger the child the less developed their internal heat regulating system, and the larger their surface area for heat dissipation in relation to their body mass.

1. Allow your children time to acclimatize. It will take them longer than it will take you. Go easy for the first few days early in the hot season or early into a trip to an area hotter than your child is used to, and increase the activity level progressively. The human body becomes increasingly able to adjust to heat.

2. Do not dress your child in clothing that traps heat. Summer clothes should be woven loosely to allow air to circulate freely over the skin and to allow moisture to evaporate freely off the skin. Snug fitting clothing restricts healthy blood circulation and should be avoided. Wearing a hat, especially one with a wide brim, shades the heat-conscious brain and the sun-sensitive face.

3. Save the hardest walking for the coolest times of the day. Around 2 P.M., when thoughtful desert dwellers are conserving their strength and moisture with a siesta, so should you and your child.

4. Do not give your child antihistamines. The stronger ones block the sympathetic nerves that stimulate sweating and predispose the child to heat problems. (Antihistamines will have the same effect on you.)

5. Monitor more closely the child who is overweight. Excess body fat reduces the ability to shed excess heat. The long and lean are heat-dissipaters while those who enjoy the cold are often fat-insulated heat-retainers.

6. If you find it difficult to get kids to drink plain water, add enough powdered flavoring to make the water less boring, but not enough to make it syrupy.

7. Know how to treat an overheated child. They need rest in the shade and a lot of fluids, especially water, to drink. Loosen any restrictive clothing. They can be sponged or splashed with water and fanned to increase the cooling rate.

Kids and dehydration. Children dehydrate faster than adults, and fluid loss, especially via diarrhea, can be devastating. One of the best and earliest signs of dehydration is urine color: clear indicates a well-hydrated child (or adult) and dark yellow indicates poor hydration. As dehydration grows worse, watch for headache, unusual fatigue, loss of appetite, nausea, and other complaints that make you think flu. One of the later signs of serious dehydration in a child is restlessness and unusual loss of interest in whatever is going on around them.

For treating diarrhea, carry a mild antidiarrheal medication in your first-aid kit. Children should continue to eat during episodes of diarrhea. Avoid milk and other dairy products for a day. Infants do well on rice cereal, applesauce, and bananas for a day or two. Older children may eat plain dry toast, plain crackers, plain chicken soup, and other bland foods.

For treating dehydration, whether from diarrhea, vomiting, or heat, use oral rehydration salts (ORS) instead of plain water. ORS replace essential salts and contain a little sugar for energy. You can buy ORS or make your own rehydration solution by adding 1 teaspoon of sugar and a pinch of salt to 1 quart of water. Do not use salt tablets.

Kids and sunshine. "The sun is even worse for children than it is for adults," says Karl Neumann, M.D., associate clinical professor of pediatrics, Cornell Medical College. Even though the damage may not show up for thirty years, 80 percent of skin damage from the sun (including skin cancers) happens in the first couple of decades of life.

Children sunburn more easily than adults. Children should wear clothing woven tight enough to protect their skin from ultraviolet (UV) light, wear hats with a brim to protect their faces, and use sunscreen on unprotected skin. Ultraviolet A and B rays damage skin, and the sunscreen should protect against both. Assume the SPF (Sun Protection Factor) is not as good as it claims and use a higher number. "Recent studies," says Dr. Neumann, "show that the new sunscreens with SPF numbers of 30 and higher are, in fact, more protective even over the first few hours of exposure." Sunscreens should be applied in a uniform coat over all exposed areas. If your journey involves swimming, use a waterproof sunscreen and reapply it often. A few inches of water will not protect your child's skin from sunburn. Once a pleasant suntan is established, the screen should still be used. Tans may prevent burning but offer little protection from the harmful effects of the sun.

Dr. Neumann suggests these further precautions: Keep children under one year out of the sun as much as possible, and apply sunscreens to their sensitive skin only when absolutely necessary. Avoid sunscreens that contain para-aminobenzoic acid (PABA). PABA is highly irritating to skin. Test the sunscreen on a small portion of skin first, about the size of the child's hand, to see if the child will react. If they do react, try a different brand. For young children, use a sunscreen prepared as a milky lotion or cream, and avoid the upper and lower eyelids where the sunscreen might be rubbed involuntarily into the eye. Never use baby oil in the sun. Encourage children to wear sunglasses in order to reduce the chance of cataracts later in life, and to protect their sensitive eyelids.

If your child gets a sunburn, start treatment as soon as possible. Cool compresses may reduce the pain and limit the depth of the burn. Pack a moisturizer, and apply it liberally. Acetaminophen may be given for pain. Drinking a lot of water is important in the treatment of sunburn.

Kids and insects. Children usually have more trouble than adults resisting the temptation to scratch itchy bites. Because they are also typically less hygienic than adults, scratches on children have a higher rate of infection. Sting wipes may be used immediately to reduce the temptation to scratch. Hydrocortisone cream will reduce the itch of more established bites. Bites that are scratched open should be washed with soap and water, and covered with an adhesive strip bandage.

For prevention, insect repellent should be used regularly. DEET, a common repelling ingredient, should not be used in a high concentration. For children the lower the concentration, the better. The safest alternative for kids is a repellent containing lemon eucalyptus oil (which will work for you, too).

Kids and cold. Children lose core temperature faster than adults. Children also tend to show poorer judgment concerning maintenance of body heat. Parents need to make sure children are dressed properly for the cold: hats that hold in heat, winter boots (not summer boots with extra socks stuffed on the feet), mittens (not gloves). On treks make sure children stay well-hydrated, eat regularly, and stay as dry as possible. Parents need to watch children closely for the tell-tale signs of hypothermia (see "Health and Safety" in On the Trail) in order to treat a problem (change into dry clothing and snuggle) before it becomes serious.

Kids and poisons. Campsites should be checked closely in order to identify the presence of poison oak, sumac, or ivy. Children should be made aware of, and taught how to identify and avoid, all plants that poison via contact. If contact is suspected, all skin that may have contacted the poisonous plant should be washed immediately with soft soap and cold water. Clothing, including shoes, that may have contacted the poisonous plant should be cleaned thoroughly. If the itch, redness, and fluid-filled bumps of a reaction to the plants develops on skin, hydrocortisone cream may be used to treat the symptoms. Only time will bring healing.

Teach kids to never eat anything unless you give it to them. Small children make up the great majority of ingested poison victims. In a suspected poisoning, you may consider inducing vomiting as soon as possible. The child should first be given at least eight ounces of water to drink. Then gently stimulate the gag reflex with your finger. Do not induce vomiting in children who are having seizures, are lethargic or in danger of further loss of consciousness, have already vomited, have ingested a corrosive substance (which usually produces burns on the lips or in the mouth), or have ingested a petroleum product. If the child has ingested a poison, he or she should be evacuated to a medical facility as soon as possible, even if vomiting has occurred.

Kids and medications. Children aged five and under usually cannot swallow pills. Carry chewable tablets. For children too young to chew, the tablets can be crushed and added to food. Some children's medications are available in liquid form, less desirable for trekking, but it might be your best choice.

Kids and ouchies. Little people get scraped and cut and blistered just like big people, but they sometimes make less than perfect patients. To encourage cooperation, carry kid-oriented wound management products such as adhesive strip bandages depicting their favorite cartoon characters.

Kids and hygiene. Baby wipes make washing up in camp a less tedious chore. (And they work great for you, too.)

Kids get lost. To help prevent children from wandering off indiscreetly into the wild places, set strict boundaries around campsites. Encourage children to hug-a-tree (stay put) if they get lost. Supply children with whistles and a code: Three blows means "Help!" . . . and two blows means "We hear you!"

> "All know that the drop merges into the ocean but few know that the ocean merges into the drop."
> *Kabir*

International Trekking

Rain fell in proverbial torrents. Hunkered down beneath broad leaves that roofed a shelter without walls, I shared my last chocolate bar with a wide-grinned Peruvian boy and his easy-going father. We had almost no words in common. We had very little difficulty communicating. Not far away clouds shrouded the ancient ruins of Machu Picchu. It remains a treasured moment.

The Peruvian Andes. The Himalaya of Nepal. The Outback of Australia. Lands wreathed in mystery, wrapped in myth, waiting to be explored. There are few reasons, and none of them very forceful, to let your treks remain inside the nation of your birth. Financially speaking, for instance, if you travel independently and frugally, the price is little more than you would spend on an across-the-country domestic vacation. Ground costs in South America, Africa, and much of Asia can be as cheap as dirt.

Passports and Visas

Before you make too many plans, make sure you have a passport, a necessity for international travel. It must be valid, and it must have space left (if you are already an avid international traveler) for new visa stamps. You need to apply for one, or apply for a renewal, an absolute minimum of at least six weeks before you plan to leave. Applications are handled by the U.S. Passport Agency, some post offices, and some state and federal courts.

Entering and leaving another country requires, in most cases, a visa. Some countries require one before you leave home, and some are issued on arrival.

European countries, exceptions to the rule, do not require visas from Americans, but much of the rest of the world does. Other variables related to visas include type, such as tourist or business, and the procedures surrounding acquiring one. As to procedures, they seem to change often, but embassies and consulates hosted by the United States are usually sources of up-to-date info. You can get the embassy's phone number from *The Statesman's Yearbook* at your library's reference desk or from the State Department at (202) 647-5225. Travel agents can be very helpful, especially if you booked your travel through them. They usually have access to online databases and/or reference works. You may be able to access references online on your own.

Health Abroad

Staying healthy abroad starts long before you step onto the plane. Allow six to eight weeks, minimum, to get everything done that will be required or recommended. As always, but even more importantly, when you leave for an international trek, start with physical and dental checkups so you can step out with all your parts in proper working order.

Vaccinations. Do not leave home without checking with your physician and/or the Centers for Disease Control (CDC) about which vaccinations to get and other health precautions to take before entering the foreign countries on your itinerary. Check the CDC website (*www.cdc.gov*) and select "Travelers' Health"—or dial their automated fax system (404) 332-4565 (press 3). Current recommendations for U.S. travelers issued by the CDC are also found in an annual publication called *Health Information for International Travel*. The publication contains vaccination and certification requirements on a country-by-country basis. It also has the U.S. Public Health Service recommendations for difficult immunization questions, such as immunization of infants, breastfeeding and pregnant women, and specific recommendations for vaccination and prophylaxis for each of a wide variety of disorders. It provides a discussion of specific potential health hazards worldwide by geographic region as well. The information in the book is updated biweekly in a publication called the *Summary of Health Information for International Travel*. Both the book and updates can be obtained from the Superintendent of Documents, U.S. Government Printing Office, Washington, DC 20402. They are also available at many libraries, and nearly all state health departments and travel clinics.

Immunizations. Travelers should make sure their childhood immunizations—including polio, measles, mumps, diphtheria, and whooping cough—are up-to-date. All travelers should be assured of their tetanus immunity, and should consider acquiring immunity to hepatitis A.

Food and water. Amoebic dysentery, diarrheal diseases, and parasitic worms—bad things that can happen to you—are associated with poor choice of water and food in many countries. Disinfect all water before drinking it or brushing your teeth with it (see "Health and Safety" in On the Trail). Avoid milk, butter, and other dairy products. Bottled drinks are usually okay, but you are safer watching them being uncapped before you accept one. All food is safer when it is well-cooked and served hot. Beware of raw vegetables, peeled fruit, salads, seafood (especially shellfish), and meat not cooked well and dished out hot. Fruits with intact skins are safe as long as you peel them shortly before eating them.

International Travel Tips

▲ Secure permits and maps in advance by contacting overseas embassies or land management offices before leaving home.

▲ Contact the State Department (*www.state.gov*) about any precautions to take. Consular information sheets (available online) explain each country's entry requirements, areas of instability, medical facilities, embassy locations, and more.

▲ Avoid the types of clothing, baggage, and other accessories that indicate you are a wealthy tourist. Conceal expensive gear and jewelry, and lock all checked luggage.

▲ Arrive at your destination early in the day so you can get out of the city quickly and to a hotel or campsite close to the trailhead. Research plane, train, bus, and rental car options in advance.

▲ Obtain some local currency before leaving home so you can pay for taxis and tips immediately upon arriving at your overseas destination.

▲ Consider hiring a guide (ask for references from friends and travel agents). In developing countries, guides can expedite your movements through crowded airports, customs, permit lines, and traffic jams. They will also know which spots to avoid.

▲ Leave your itinerary (including a photocopy of your passport) with family or friends back home.

▲ Do not worry about language barriers. English is spoken widely, surprisingly widely. And you accomplish much by just smiling and being polite. But you will enjoy learning a few local words such as *please, thank you, sorry, yes, no, hello, goodbye, food, water, toilet, sleep, help,* and *how much* (does it cost)?

▲ Customize your first-aid kit. Your doctor might be willing to prescribe drugs to manage pain and local diseases that have no vaccination. Consider sterile syringes in case you need an injection.

▲ Take out a travel insurance policy and make sure it covers medical expenses outside the United States.

Foreign Cultures

Trekking provides the rare and precious opportunity to travel the trails with locals. This type of experience includes mingling with people who might have vastly different cultural values, social mores, and religious beliefs that govern the lives of individuals, families, and societies. There may be, in other words, things that are acceptable and things that are unacceptable—and there will always be wonderful things to learn. Courtesy and respect will carry you successfully a long way past mistakes, and a keen and friendly interest will often open doors of hospitality and learning that will deepen your own life appreciably. You might find your life-deepening experiences enhanced by learning as much as possible before you set foot on foreign soil (see Appendix B).

Conditioning for the Long Trail

Only one thing separates those folks who walk the long trail and those whose wilderness jaunts are limited to weekends: Desire. Just about anybody can get in shape for multitudes of miles. There is no special body-build or age-group better suited for extended treks. It is the mind that makes the difference.

Cardiovascular Training

With aerobic workouts, the heart grows more efficient, pushing more blood with every pump, and pumping it more easily. Capillaries, where oxygen and nutrients pass from the blood into muscle cells, increase in number, and the cells themselves grow better at using the fuel you are sending their way. Those beneficial changes start immediately. In fact, you can get a 10 percent jump in the amount of blood pushed in one beat with a few short jogs or bike rides.

Although it used to be thought that the more you worked out the greater the benefits, that just is not necessarily so. Truth is, working out four days a week is plenty for almost everyone. How fast your level of cardiovascular fitness increases is determined by how intensely you work out. Intensity is measured by how fast your heart beats during exercise. The fastest gains will be made when you exercise at an intensity level of about 80 percent of your maximum heart rate. Maximum heart rate is found by subtracting your age from 220. This formula is not precise, but it does give you a good idea of how hard you can safely work out for best cardiovascular results.

And, speaking of safety, it is easy to overdo it. Start with no more than one short, intense workout a week combined with 3 days of light exercise. Increase the length of intensity as you feel more capable. Intensity can be increased by adding speed (go faster) or adding effort (go uphill). When you can do one forty-minute high-intensity workout, start building toward a second one, with a rest day in between, until you can do four a week.

What kind of cardiovascular exercise is best to train for the long trail? Nothing gets you in shape for walking long miles with a heavy pack better than walking long miles with a heavy pack. But to endure and, more importantly, enjoy the long trail, a cardiovascular exercise program is a must. What you do aerobically is not nearly

The hardest part of exercise is opening the front door (Stan Swartz).

as important as doing something. The hardest part of any exercise program is opening the front door.

Strength Training

Legs and hips are the muscular motivating factors. Under the load of a heavy pack, you also use the muscles of your back and buttocks, as well as those of your neck and shoulders. Your knees and ankles also take a beating. If you have the time, and the get-up-and-go, preparation for the long trail should include some weight-lifting in order to strengthen the specific body parts you will be using.

Remember, you are not trying to hurt yourself or end up looking like a body builder. Choose a weight with which you can do eight to ten repetitions on the first set with enough energy left to do one or two more sets after a brief rest of about 45 seconds. Lift the weights slowly and steadily, using good form, and thinking about the specific muscles you are exercising. Three workouts a week with rest days in between will be enough.

Flexibility Training

Incorporate ten minutes of daily stretching exercises into your workout plan. Stretching should be slow and gentle, not ballistic, a good way to relax after a workout (see "Stretching for Peace" in On the Trail).

Start every workout with about ten minutes of warm-up to avoid muscle strains. You can jog slowly or walk briskly, but aggressive stretching is not recommended.

Back squats. With the barbell resting across the upper back, drop slowly until your thighs are parallel to the floor and, without stopping, rise steadily back to a standing position, but do not lock your knees. Heels should remain in contact with the floor. This is an important exercise for strengthening most of your backpacking muscles and building coordination.

Leg press. To do this exercise requires a leg press machine. If one is available, the benefits to the front of your thigh muscles can be tremendous. Lower the weight slowly, taking care to not bounce the weight as your knees drop toward your chest. Push the weight up steadily, and, once again, do not lock your knees.

Leg curls. This exercise also requires a machine, and strengthens the back of your thigh. As you curl the weight up, tighten your abdominals and buttocks for additional benefit.

Abdominal crunches. Lie on your back with your knees bent at 90 degrees and your lower legs parallel to the floor. Push your lower back toward the floor as you curl your head and shoulders toward your knees. If you do these right, you do not have to do very many before your abs start to burn. It is very important to concentrate on your stomach muscles as you do crunches. This exercise is critical for protecting your lower back and tying your lower back muscles to your upper back muscles.

Seated press. Working directly on the shoulders, the seated press should be started with the bar across the upper chest. Push it straight up, keeping your back straight, and lower it slowly back down to the starting position. Vary how far apart you spread your hands on the bar.

Shoulder shrugs. With bar held in front of your body, arms hanging down, try to touch your shoulders to your ears. This strengthens the muscles that bear the direct load of your pack.

Dips. This is a great exercise if you have dip bars or a dip station on a weight machine. It does for the upper body things similar to what squats do for the lower body. Start with your arms straight, your legs bent, and your chin on your chest. Drop slowly and push straight up powerfully. This works your chest, but also strengthens your shoulders and the backs of your arms.

Pullups. To maximize back strengthening, palms should be facing away from you. To minimize the chance of over-stressing your elbows, keep them slightly flexed when you are hanging from the bar. Vary how far apart you spread your hands on the bar on this one, too.

The Stuff of Endurance

So you want more endurance. Getting more oomph out of a long day under a heavy load means you have packed your body with the same care with which you packed your backpack. Start before you hit the trail.

Glycogen is the first fuel your body burns for endurance. Glycogen was once the food you ate, derived from carbohydrates and strung now, like pearls, into

Daily stretching keeps you ready to trek (Alan Bauer).

chains of glucose molecules. Built from your diet of the last 24 hours or so, glycogen waits, packed into the cells of your muscles and liver, ready to provide energy. What you have eaten prior to the hike, and your level of physical fitness, determines how long you will endure.

Energy production takes place within each of your muscle cells. For the first twenty to thirty minutes of your hiking day, stored muscle glycogen provides almost your entire source of energy, with the addition of a little glucose from your blood which has been released from the stores in your liver. But the drain on your glycogen starts to tell. Hormone levels in your blood change, insulin lowering and epinephrine rising, and stored fats begin to play an increasing role in providing energy. At the ninety-minute mark for the average trekker, fats and blood glucose have become a major supplier of endurance. With 2 hours behind you, glycogen has almost been used up. Fortunately, your fat supply is virtually inexhaustible. Unfortunately, fats will not burn unless carbohydrates are present, and continued exercise depends on your muscles taking glucose from your blood. You must take on more carbs or you start to poop out.

Replenishing carbs can be accomplished effectively with a drink containing a 6–7 percent concentration of carbohydrates. Within minutes glucose will be spilling into your bloodstream. Higher concentrations are absorbed more sluggishly, sometimes causing an upset stomach. For optimum endurance, drinks should be taken in small swallows consistently throughout periods of exercise at a rate of about a liter per hour. Start sipping around thirty minutes into your hike to avoid carb depletion.

If you do not like carb-replacement drinks, endurance can be maintained with energy bars, candy bars, and other trail snacks. They will take thirty to sixty minutes to kick into action, and they must be followed with the same drinking regimen using plain water. Even if you are using drinks for carbohydrates, you should still start munching something about ninety minutes into your exercise, to ensure your blood glucose stays high enough to prevent exhaustion. When energy stores are exhausted, they take a long time, up to a day, to rebuild.

Another reason exists for keeping your carb intake adequate. After 2 hours of strenuous backpacking without taking the time to replenish carbohydrates, your brain, which feeds almost entirely off blood glucose, may begin to complain with headaches and dizziness. Your ability to think things through carefully will rapidly diminish. You may find yourself in serious trouble.

To maintain energy stores within your muscles, the normal American diet of approximately 46 percent carbohydrates is not enough. A diet containing 70 percent carbohydrates is recommended when you are exercising hard. Here is a healthy suggestion: Balance your diet, as much as possible, from the four food groups—dairy, proteins, fruits and vegetables, and grains—then double your intake of fruits and vegetables, and triple your intake of grains to achieve a high-carb diet.

Primary carbohydrate sources are cereals, breads, pastas, muffins, pancakes, rolls, rice and other grain products, fruits, and vegetables.

For food to be burned into energy, oxygen must be present in each cell. The harder you work, the more oxygen you use. But you, and everyone else, will reach a place during exercise beyond which your ability to use oxygen will not increase, even if the intensity of your exercise continues to rise. When you are using oxygen at your maximum capacity, you have reached an exercise plateau of 100 percent aerobic capacity. You can only function at maximum for about five minutes. Then you will reach another poop-out point. Training for endurance will increase your ability to use oxygen. That, in practical terms, means you will be able to cover the same distance on the trail with less effort, or a greater distance with the same effort.

Water, believe it or not, is the most commonly overlooked endurance aid. Even very mild dehydration produces a loss of efficiency. Before heading out along the trail, drink a half-liter of cold water. Cold fluids empty from the stomach quicker and cool the engine, preparing it for the heat stress of the exercise to come. Once you are on the trail, keep up the consistent drinking—plain water or energy drink—at the rate of approximately a liter per hour (see "Health and Safety" in On the Trail).

PART 3
On the Trail

Your feet are finally setting down, one in front of the other, on the trek. Miles and miles, days and, perhaps, weeks lie ahead of you. The attention you have given to planning ahead and preparing will pay off. But there are still details, many details, that, if you consider them now, will add to your comfort, enjoyment, and safety—and to the preservation of that wildland that holds so much attraction and deserves so much care.

Leave No Trace

Everyone, or at least almost everyone, who loves the wilderness desires a wilderness experience. A large part of that experience lies in finding the wildland not only wild but also uncluttered, unaffected by other human visitors. Finding it that way can be deeply satisfying personally, but your visit can be costly to the places visited and the animals observed. In some areas we are indeed loving the wilderness to death.

Wildland can be extremely fragile. Pollution of water sources, erosion of soils, and trampling of vegetation are just some of the impacts linked directly to recreational activities. Even the simple fact that you are there has an influence. Considerable damage can be prevented if wilderness users are better informed, especially about Leave No Trace techniques. But true preservation results not just from knowing how to act but from acting appropriately.

At the heart of Leave No Trace are not only ethical beliefs but also seven principles for reducing the damage caused by outdoor activities, particularly non-motorized recreation. Leave No Trace principles and practices extend common courtesy and hospitality to nature and to other wildland visitors. They are based on respect for nature and the science behind leaving no trace.

Plan Ahead and Prepare

Plan ahead by considering your goals and expectations and taking pretrip steps to preserve the wild places. Prepare by gathering information and skills. Plan to Leave No Trace and prepare by learning how to Leave No Trace. Plan, for instance, by reducing the amount of garbage you carry by repackaging food, getting rid of trash you might accidentally leave behind. Prepare by learning specific minimum impact techniques for the area you are visiting. A desert needs respect in ways that differ from subalpine meadows. It is your responsibility to Leave No Trace.

Leave No Trace Principles

1. Plan ahead and prepare.
2. Travel and camp on durable surfaces.
3. Dispose of waste properly.
4. Leave what you find.
5. Minimize campfire impacts.
6. Respect wildlife.
7. Be considerate of other visitors.

Travel and Camp on Durable Surfaces

Litter is ugly but is easily picked up. Trampled vegetation and eroded trails, on the other hand, might last for years—or a lifetime. Choose to set your feet and your tent on surfaces that endure: rock, sand, gravel, dry grasses, sedges, snow, or water.

Above tree line, spread a group out to minimize the impact to the environment (NOLS/Deborah Sussex.

Proper management of human waste prevents the spread of disease and eliminates the ugliness (NOLS/Goodrich).

In popular areas, concentrate your use where it is obvious other visitors have already left an impact. Stay on trails, avoid shortcuts, use established campsites and fire rings. Good campsites, says the old maxim, are found, not made. And leave your campsite as clean and natural looking as possible.

In pristine areas without noticeable impact, disperse your use. When you travel off-trail, walk on durable surfaces and avoid creating obvious campsites. Groups should not walk in single file, trampling the earth into a visible pathway. Spend no more than one night at a pristine site.

Dispose of Waste Properly

Despite your familiarity with the expression, it is worth repeating: "Pack it in, pack it out." Inspect your campsites and your rest-break spots, and leave nothing behind. Carry garbage bags and pack out leftover food as well as your trash. And lend a hand by packing out the refuse discarded by others.

Dispose of your human waste thoughtfully and appropriately. Use outhouses if they are available. Otherwise dig a cat hole 6- to 8- inches deep at least 200 feet (about 70 adult steps) from water, camp, trails, and drainages. If you choose to use toilet paper, pack it out. Urinate well away from camps and trails on rocks or bare ground rather than on vegetation. Where water is plentiful, consider diluting the urine by rinsing the site.

To wash your dishes and cookware, carry water 200 feet away from streams or lakes. Strain dirty dishwater with a fine mesh strainer (or an old nylon stocking will do) before scattering the dirty water. Pack out the material left in the strainer.

Soap, even biodegradable soap, can affect the water quality of lakes and streams, so minimize its use. Always wash yourself at least 200 feet from shorelines, and rinse with water carried in a pot. Consider using a hand sanitizer that allows you to wash your hands without worrying about wastewater disposal (see "Health and Safety," later in this section).

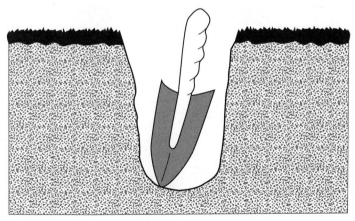

A cat hole needs to be 6- to 8-inches deep.

Leave What You Find

Sometimes what you do not see creates the most disturbing impact of a wilderness trek. Archeological and historical artifacts are reminders of the rich human history of America, and they belong to all people for all time. Structures, dwellings, and artifacts on public lands are protected by the Archaeological Resources Protection Act and the National Historic Preservation Act, and should not be disturbed. Do not pick the flowers, collect the rocks, or take the deer antlers home to decorate your office wall. If you want a souvenir, take a photo, draw a picture, and cherish the memories.

Minimize Campfire Impacts

The lasting impacts of traditional open fires can be avoided by using lightweight stoves. If fires are acceptable, build a minimum impact fire—use an existing fire ring, a mound fire, or a fire pan. Use only dead and downed wood, nothing bigger around than your wrist, keep the fire small, burn all the wood down to ash, saturate the ash with water, and scatter the ash broadly. Get rid of all evidence of your fire.

Mound fires leave no scars on the land (NOLS).

Respect Wildlife

Although some wild animals adapt to human presence, others flee, sometimes abandoning their young and their preferred habitat. Observe quietly from a distance. Avoid quick movements and direct eye contact, actions that may be interpreted as aggression. And do not, intentionally or unintentionally—by leaving trash or insecurely storing food—feed wildlife. If you must travel with your pet, make sure that local regulations allow it and make sure your pet is under control at all times (see "Trail Companions" in Before You Go).

Be Considerate of Other Visitors

Yes, you own the wilderness, along with millions of others. And they, too, deserve respect. The little things are often the most important. Simple courtesies such as offering a friendly greeting on the trail, wearing earth-toned clothing to blend in with the environment, stepping aside to let someone pass, waiting patiently for a turn, or preserving the quiet, all make a difference. Practice trail etiquette. Hikers should move to the downhill side and talk quietly to horseback riders as they pass. Before passing others, politely announce your presence and proceed with caution. Lend a hand, if appropriate, to help those ahead. Take rest breaks on durable surfaces a short distance (but out of sight when possible) from the trail. If possible, camp out of sight and sound of trails and other visitors.

Maintaining Self on the Trail

Too often you forget, I forget, we forget that the body and the mind are inseparable. When asked what you want out of life, your almost thoughtless response is often peace of mind. You do not need to think about it because the answer is instinctive. Far less instinctive is the fact that the mind typically fails to find peace when the body is uptight. Perhaps that explains at least one reason why the long trail beckons so many of us.

You and I need the peace of wild places, but it does not come as soon as we step away from the car. It takes a few days of "leaving behind" to reach that peaceful state of mind. Why? Part of the problem is our inability to switch our state of mind on and off. Peace, like Siddhartha's river, flows in and out of our lives. Part of the problem is our too sedentary lives. It takes time for legs to accept the trail and our shoulders to accept the pack.

Stretching for Peace

Stretching is the most important physical link between the sedentary life and the active life. When done regularly, it keeps muscles supple. Although a few gentle stretches to loosen up in the morning are beneficial, it is better to save a stretching workout for the evening. Too much stretching before hitting the trail may actually weaken your muscles, and starting out slowly on the trail will warm up and loosen

A Specific Stretching Routine

The calves. Face a rock or tree and lean forward to place your forearms against the rock or tree. Put your hands together and rest your forehead against your hands. Keep your toes pointing straight toward the support. Flex one knee and shift your foot toward the support. Your back leg should be straight with your heel flat. Without changing foot position shift your hips slightly forward until you create the easy feeling of stretch in your calf. When one calf is stretched, switch to the other one.

The groin. Sit down. Put the bottoms of your feet together and hold them there with your hands. Keep your heels a comfortable distance from your groin. Gently pull your upper body forward until you feel the stretch in your groin. Keep your lower back straight, not rounded, and keep your head up. Remember: mild tension, hold until it goes away, breathe slowly, repeat.

The hamstrings. Remain sitting. Straighten out one leg and keep the other curled into your groin. Bend forward from your hips along your outstretched leg with your head neutral and your lower back straight. Do not "lock" your knee straight. Keep it slightly flexed. Be sure to keep your upper thigh muscles (quadriceps) relaxed. Do not try to touch your head to your knee. Remember to keep your upper body relaxed. After stretching one leg, switch leg positions, and repeat.

Now lie back slowly, stretch your arms over your head, and make your body as long as you possibly can. Breathe in deeply while you elongate yourself. This feels really great. Pull one knee toward your chest and hold. Repeat with the other leg. It may not feel like you are stretching much, but you are relaxing your whole body. When you are finished, roll onto your side for a few moments before standing up.

The shoulder. While standing erect, roll your shoulders in full circles with your arms dangling relaxed at your side—up to your ears, forward, down, back. Reverse the motion. Now add your arms, slowly swinging them in full swimming motions forward a few circles, and backward a few circles. While maintaining an erect posture, clasp your hands behind your back. Keep your arms almost straight and lean forward slowly from your hips, lifting your arms toward the sky.

you for the day's exercise. In addition, stretching helps prevent injury. Stretching is easy, but it can do harm if done incorrectly. It should be relaxing and noncompetitive and, well, peaceful.

The fibers of your muscles have a built-in stretch reflex. You can pull them just so far and then they contract for protection. Stretching too far too fast will actually counteract the beneficial effect you are after. The correct way to stretch is in a relaxed, sustained movement with your attention focused on the muscles being stretched. The incorrect way is to bounce up and down with your mind wandering or stretching to the point of pain.

Begin each stretch with 10–30 seconds of mild tension. As soon as you feel the tension in the muscle, stop the stretch, and hold that position. This easy stretch will reduce muscular tightness and prepare tissues for the developmental stretch.

When you feel the mild tension ease off, move slightly forward until it returns and hold that new position for 10–30 seconds, until the tension diminishes. Try counting softly to yourself as you hold the stretch until the feeling becomes natural and you no longer need to count. Be aware of your breathing. Exhale as you bend forward. During the period of stretch-holding, breathe slowly and rhythmically.

Do not stretch merely to increase flexibility. Several things are more important to you than becoming more limber: Keep all your muscles relaxed—feet and hands, fingers and toes, neck and shoulders—during the stretch. Remember your body will not be exactly the same on any 2 days. It will even vary between morning and night. Adjust your stretch to the way your body presents itself. Never try to force it to be the way it was the last time you met it for a stretch. Keep your body properly aligned during a stretch to maximize the event. Learn to get the right "feel" out of a stretch instead of seeing how far you can go.

Fatigue-Free Hiking

Once upon a time there was this rabbit that ran really fast, exhausted himself, and lost the Big Race to a turtle who plodded along at a steady unpretentious pace. This fable of Aesop's overruns with educational opportunities, but one important lesson is this: You do not have to hike until you're pooped out and throw yourself down at the end of the day worn out and aching and wondering if you should have stayed home and watched TV.

Turtles move unhurriedly through life, pack their tent and sleeping bag everywhere they go, carry enough food to last for months, and live a long time. To the ancient Greeks they were a symbol of wisdom. They are additionally a symbol of fatigue-free trekking.

Everything you do requires energy (see "The Stuff of Endurance" in Before You Go). To backpack fatigue-free means to conserve your energy as much as possible. Rabbits zip along, stop and pant, zip along, stop and pant. Turtles never stop to catch their breath because their breath never gets away from them. Nothing indicates how fast you are expending your trail energy more than your rate of breathing. Instead of letting your pace control your breathing and puffing like a burned-out bunny, let your breathing control your pace. For example, on even terrain you might breathe in for every two or three steps you take, and breathe out on the next two or three. When the trail grows steeper and you feel the need for more air, slow down and take one or two steps for each inhalation and one or two steps for each exhalation. If the trail gets really steep, you might eventually end up taking one step for each in-and-out breath. Rest breaks should be taken to rest your muscles, not to catch your breath. After practicing, rhythmic breathing will become second nature, and over-fatigue will become a thing of the past.

If you reach a point where you feel the need for more oxygen, make your exhalations against pursed lips, the sort of lips you make when you blow out a candle. Pursed-lip breathing creates a little back pressure on your airway causing the oxygen-absorbing areas of your lungs to increase oxygen uptake. You will get a bit more "oomph" out of each breath.

The speed at which you move on down the trail depends on your level of fitness. As your fitness improves, your pace will increase. As another indication of your pace matching your fitness, take the talk test. If you can hike and maintain a conversation, you are hiking at an acceptable pace for your level of fitness. If you cannot talk and hike at the same time, you are over-fatiguing yourself.

You never see a turtle going straight uphill. The shortest distance between two points may be a straight line, but going straight up a hillside produces quick fatigue. That fact at least partially explains why maintained trails have switchbacks, sharp turns back and forth across the fall line. When hiking in steep country without trails, follow a zigzag pattern. Switchbacking makes for longer travel time, but it conserves the most energy.

Without a trail to follow on steep terrain, reduce fatigue even more by sidehill-gouging as you traverse the hillside. Instead of placing your foot flat on the angle of the ground, which rolls your ankle downhill, kick your foot slightly into the dirt or snow to create a partial platform to step on. It takes far less energy to walk with your ankles straight. If you are wearing fairly stiff-soled boots, sidehill-gouging tends to be more successful.

Conserve more energy on really steep terrain by using the rest-step. In the rest-step, your downhill leg should be kept straight so your bones support your weight and not your tense muscles. When your uphill foot has found a secure place to stand, straighten your uphill leg, roll forward, and rest your weight on your "new" downhill leg. The rest-step, not a natural way to walk, needs to become an act of discipline. The momentary rests you give your leg muscles may not seem beneficial, but after thousands of steps they become significant.

The length of your stride depends on the length of your leg. As long as your stride feels comfortable, it is probably the best stride for you. But shorten your stride while hiking uphill—taking shorter steps while ascending requires less effort. It takes more energy to climb stairs taking two steps at a time. It takes more energy to climb hills with long strides than short strides.

All uphill trails lead to downhill trails, and going downhill increases the punishment on your body. Knees crunch under the impact, ankles may twist, muscles and tendons and ligaments get loads of stress. Shorter steps produce less stress on joints and muscles than long downhill steps. Careful foot placement helps reduce the chance you will lose your balance (and possibly get injured) on rocks, limbs, and uneven ground—and it takes a burst of energy to regain your balance.

When steep slopes are covered with snow, loose dirt, pebbly scree, or rocks smaller than your fist, you can point your toes downhill and shuffle along in a sort of skiing motion, a technique called "glissading" (see "The Land of White," later in this section). If your balance is good, you can glissade down long distances in a short time with very little energy consumption.

If glissading is not an option, sidehill-gouging and switchbacking conserve energy going down just as they do going up.

> ### Shouldering the Pack
>
> Every time you shoulder your pack, you use up a chunk of energy. The most energy-conserving method of getting a pack on your back requires a second person, someone to lift the pack while you slip into it. Second-best is lifting the pack onto a waist-high rock or embankment, slipping into the straps, leaning forward, and hiking away. If these methods are not available, grab the shoulder straps and pull the pack up your lower leg onto your knee and thigh muscles. Then hold onto the left shoulder strap with your left hand and shove your right arm and shoulder into the strap while simultaneously twisting your back into the pack. Slip in your left shoulder, tighten the straps and hipbelt, and you are ready to go.

Clothes that restrict your movement decrease comfort and increase your workload. Your choice of pants is particularly important. Generally, the lightest and loosest pants offer the most energy conservation. Short pants in warmer weather help keep you cool, which also helps keep you stronger. In colder weather, loose-fitting layers on the lower half of your body create dead air space trapping heat and allowing you to use your energy for motion instead of unnecessary body heat maintenance. Layers allow you to peel off one or two when you get too hot. The more you assist your body in maintaining a normal core temperature, the more energy you will have for other activities.

Other Fatigue Preventing Steps

▲ Walk around obstacles, not over them. Do not step up onto logs, rocks, or bumps in the terrain when you can step over or walk around the obstacles. It takes more energy to step up, and a long day of stepping up can add many feet of unnecessary elevation gain and loss.

▲ Watch the trail ahead, and plan your steps to avoid obstacles.

▲ Walk flat-footed on steep trails when the terrain allows it. It requires less energy to plant your feet flatly and use your large thigh muscles for movement than to overuse your calf muscles by rolling often from heel to toe.

- If you do not use a trekking pole or poles, swing your arms periodically to restore circulation.
- If you do not use trekking poles, periodically hike with your hands on your hips. This relieves a little stress in your lower back and allows your chest to inflate easier for some fatigue-easing deep breaths.
- Since the fuel to energize movement comes from the food you eat, carry ready-to-munch snacks in an easy-to-reach place. Do not let yourself get hungry.
- Water is essential for food use and energy. Drink it regularly on the trail, and never, never let yourself get dry enough to feel thirsty. When you lose one and a half liters of body fluid through sweating, not hard to do going uphill under a pack, you may reduce your energy as much as 22 percent (see "Hydration," later in this section).
- Take rest breaks often. Even if you do not feel like taking a break, rest restores energy and leaves you more rested at the end of the day.

> "The map is
> not the territory."
> *Alfred Korzbybski*

Navigation

Daniel Boone said he had never been lost, but he had, he continued, once been a mite unsure where he was for a month or so. You will probably be on a tighter schedule, and being lost ranks high among the things trekkers had rather not do. There is no big secret to staying found: You just have to know where you are at all times. An accomplished trekker carries at least the basic navigational skills. If you lack those skills, you will gain more from this section by getting out a USGS map and a compass, and matching the words in this book to your navigational tools.

The map. Unless a section of your trek takes you off-trail, you can get by, in most cases, consulting your map now and then, reminding yourself approximately where you are. Anyone with a general awareness of north can orient a map for casual use. With it oriented, you can identify many topographical features—such as nearby peaks and lakes—and determine which way to turn at unmarked trail junctions.

The contour lines swirling across a topo map connect points of equal elevation. They provide additional useful information: your approximate elevation (if you know approximately where you are), the elevation left to gain or lose between you and your destination, and the shape of natural features (which helps you identify them). The spaces between contour lines are called contour intervals, and they represent the vertical distance between the lines. Every fifth contour line is a darker color, and, somewhere on that line, you will find a number telling you the actual elevation above sea level the line represents. The accuracy of contour lines, however,

Maps tell you where you want to go . . . if you know where you are (NOLS/Tom Bol).

depends on how far apart they are—and not all maps are the same. If 500 feet separate two darker lines, as an example, and four lighter lines stand between the darker lines, separating the space between the darker lines into five sections, then the contour interval for that map is 100 feet. Contour intervals may be as short as 10 feet. The smaller the intervals, the greater the detail. With large intervals, significant terrain changes may not show on the map. (Note: Some maps list elevations in meters. One meter equals 3.3 feet.)

The compass. A compass is graduated into 360 degrees with north at 0 and at 360. The degrees are printed on a rotating dial (and if they are not, you need another compass). The compass base plate does not rotate—and it should have at least one line, called the direction arrow, that will point, more often than not, in the direction you will hike when navigating with a compass. The needle has an end that is red or orange, and an end that is white or black. The bright end of the needle points always toward magnetic north, not true north—but that only matters when more definitive navigation skills are required. A bearing is one of the 360-degree directions of the compass, and they are always taken clockwise from north. That puts east at 90 degrees, south at 180 degrees, and so forth. You are wise to choose a map as accurate as you can find. Not so with a compass. A four-degree error in a compass, for instance, will put you 368 feet off a straight line after 1 mile. That degree of error is insignificant to the average, and above average, trekker—so you can get by with an inexpensive compass.

With map and compass. The first step is deciding approximately where you are on the map. You will know this if you have been paying attention since you left your vehicle. Then you need to orient the map accurately to north. Arrows on the map itself will point the direction of true north and magnetic north relative to the map.

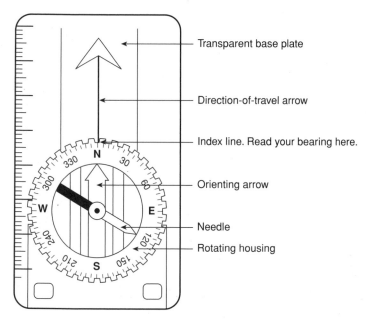

The parts of a compass

Your job is to hold the map flat with the arrow on the map pointed to true north. Do this by laying your compass on the map with the long side of the compass aligned with the arrow indicating magnetic north on the map. Make sure the north-south lines and the arrow of the rotating dial on the compass point in the same direction as the base plate's direction arrow. Now you have all the lines—the map's magnetic north line, the north-south lines on the compass, the arrow on the dial of the compass—pointing the same way. Then rotate the compass and map together until the red half of the needle sits squarely inside the faceplate arrow. Your map is now accurately oriented to true north.

Once the map is oriented, terrain features—ridges, peaks, cliffs—that you see on it lie in the same places relative to your position on the map as those features actually lie in relation to where you are actually standing. Now you can decide exactly where you are.

Off-trail. If you leave the trail, you may have to follow a bearing on your compass to up your chances of successfully arriving at your destination.

True North vs. Magnetic North

True north is the direction from you to the terrestrial North Pole. Magnetic north is the direction from you to the magnetic north pole, determined by the earth's magnetic field and located in Arctic Canada, south of the North Pole. The needle of your compass, a magnet, points to magnetic north. The angle of declination is the angle of difference between the direction of true north and the direction of magnetic north. It is read in the 360 degrees of a circle.

Basic navigational skills are a necessity for trekkers (NOLS/Deborah Sussex).

To follow a compass bearing, follow this procedure:

1. Set the compass on the map with the base plate's direction arrow lined up between where you are on the map and where you want to go.

2. Rotate the dial until the colored end of the needle is inside the north-south arrow on the faceplate, and the needle and north-south arrow are pointing in the same direction. The north-south arrow on the faceplate of the compass is now pointing to magnetic north. And now you can put the map away.

3. With the compass held flat in your hand, the base plate direction arrow will point you toward your destination while you walk, provided you keep the north-south arrow on the face plate pointing to magnetic north.

When you are following a bearing, you may run into an insurmountable obstacle such as a cliff. You need to get around it and back on your bearing—and this is not that big a deal. Start by noting the compass bearing of the direction you have to travel to get around the obstacle. As you travel in that new direction, count your steps or otherwise guess at the distance you are hiking. Once past the obstacle, reverse the distance you traveled off-course, following the exact reverse bearing to the direction you just walked off-course. If, for instance, you walked east (a bearing of 90) to get past the obstacle, you will walk back west (a bearing of 270) to get back to your original line of travel. Now you can return to following your original bearing to reach your destination.

The Art of Being Lost—and Found

▲ Do not leave on your trek without telling someone you trust where you are going and a realistic time for your return. Give this someone a copy of your itinerary, and make sure he or she knows who to contact to initiate a search-and-rescue operation. Those responsible for search-and-rescue vary from area to area, and valuable time can be saved if the right person is contacted immediately.

▲ Carry more food and clothing than you think you will need—at all times. Prepare for the worst possible conditions ever known for your chosen geographic area at your chosen time of year.

▲ Learn how to use a map and compass, and carry them at all times.

▲ If you become disoriented, recognize that you have a problem. Sit down for a half-hour and evaluate your circumstances as calmly as possible. Hasty movement burns up life-sustaining energy and creates panic. Panic is your greatest enemy. A positive attitude is your greatest tool for survival. Empty the contents of your pack and pockets, and inventory what you have with you. Mentally retrace your steps. You will probably realize your situation is not as critical as it seemed at first.

▲ It is no crime to be lost. Once you know it, stay in the immediate vicinity. Do not wander. Wandering most often will take you out of the geographic area in which the search for you will take place.

▲ Without shelter, your chance of surviving an unexpected night out is minimal in extreme environments such as severe cold. If there is nothing else available, bury yourself in leaves, pine needles, or other forest debris. In snow, burrow a hole just big enough for your body. The smaller a shelter, the more easily it is heated by your body.

▲ If possible, start a fire. Learn what natural materials will work best for fires in your area of travel. Fires are a heat-giving, light-giving, and psychological comfort-giving companion to the lost. In an emergency, a fire may substitute for shelter.

▲ Find water. Your body will suffer first from exposure and second from lack of water. Water is required for mental and physical energy.

▲ Signal your position. Bright fires at night and smoky fires during the day may alert searchers. Sets of three signals are a universal appeal for help: three fires, three blasts on a whistle, three shots from a gun, three flashes from a signal mirror. If a clearing is nearby, indicate your position to air searchers by building the largest arrow possible out of whatever is available pointing to your location. Stamp out an arrow in snow. Brightly colored outdoor clothing and gear laid on the ground or hung from a tree make very visible markers.

▲ If you run out of food, do not eat unless you can positively identify wild, nutritional edibles. The chance of eating something unsafe is great. It takes 3–5 days before hunger becomes a real problem, and much longer for it to become a life-threatening problem.

▲ Do not go onto the trail thinking "Being lost is something that will never happen to me."

When you are following a compass bearing in rough terrain, such as steep mountains, you can find yourself severely challenged. You may have to dodge around numerous obstacles, or you may hit a dead end. Your best bet is to stay tuned to specific landmark features in the distance, and take your bearings off them.

To keep a steady line off-trail in open terrain, taking a bearing off distant points such as rock outcrops or patches of vegetation should be your standard operating procedure. Remember, however, that a compass indicates only direction. When used in combination with a map, both tools will tell you exactly where you are, and in what direction you should go.

GPS. Satellites circling the earth pick up signals from a Global Positioning System device. When the signal is received by three satellites, the device displays your position on its screen. It can tell you where you are in latitude and longitude, or by using other coordinate systems, of which you will have a choice. With data from at least four satellites, a GPS can also give you a pretty good estimate of your altitude. It will work despite the worst weather and in most landscapes (although some land features may block the signals). Depending on the model you choose, a GPS may be able to do its job in seconds, store hundreds of locations, relate your average speed and distance, and even point you in the direction you wish to go if you programmed that location in earlier. Some can store a topographical map and display it on the screen. They are small enough to weigh less than a pound, usually, and fit into a pocket. On the downside, they require batteries (that, of course, can die), and they will not be the least expensive item in your pack. Do you need one? You decide.

The Obstacles of Nature

When the trail disappears, either because you left it or because the vagaries of unpredictable nature have buried it, travel requires more thought and care: Thought for your safety, and care for the environment.

The Land Above the Trees

From the edge of it, the terrain above tree line usually looks easy, but crossing it may present unusual challenges for you and the land under your feet.

Alpine tundra. The zone of life above tree line is the land of mosses, lichens, and carpets of wildflowers no higher than your ankle bones. Without a trail, walk on exposed rocks or hardy grasses, and spread out a group to avoid creating a trail (see "Leave No Trace," earlier in this section). Do not go straight up steep slopes where your footfalls may tear holes in soft ground. Instead, switchback on the most durable surfaces you can find.

Arctic tundra. In the far north, the open treeless terrain may be far more difficult to cross than you imagine. Beware those gentle-looking fields of tussocks—

unstable mounds of grass—and the surprisingly mucky wet trenches that may surround them. To avoid ankle-twisting tussock fields, traverse well-drained slopes, riverbanks, and low patches of willow where you will find drier, easier hiking. Subtle color patterns—bands of light brown bordering bands of even lighter brown—on nearby hills may reveal hiker-friendly, tussock-free zones. Wildlife trails may also come to your rescue. With no way of avoiding a field of tussocks, plan on taking a lot more time to hike across and step carefully between the mounds. Stepping on the mounds sends your risk of injury skyrocketing.

> "No snowflake falls in an inappropriate place."
> *Zen saying*

The Land of White

Far enough north (or south) and high enough up, you will find snow in every season of the year. Crossing it does not necessarily create a big problem—although it can—but several steps can be taken to make travel easier and safer.

As any winter trekker can tell you, snow comes in a wide variety of cold and white. The most important variables to you concern the water content of snow and the temperature of the snow, both of which are closely related. Very dry snow may hold as little as 5 percent water while really wet snow may contain up to 25 percent water. Snow that falls at temperatures near the freezing point can weigh three times as much as snow falling at colder temperatures because it has a much higher water content.

Dry snow (powder) is generally better for traveling until its depth reaches the point where you are struggling to make headway. After a heavy snowfall of light powder, it may take a day or two for the snow to consolidate enough to keep you on top with skis or snowshoes. It may be spring before it consolidates enough to support your weight without skis or snowshoes.

Wet snow not only gets you wet, but it adds considerably to your traveling difficulty. Wet snow sticks to skis, snowshoes, crampons, and sometimes boots. Since wet snow falls when the temperature is relatively warm, it is also difficult to keep from overheating underneath your raingear when you are huffing along under a pack. Coastal areas typically receive wet snow, and inland areas receive much drier snow, but snowfalls early in the season in any region can be wet.

Whiteouts. Mountain clouds sometimes appear out of thin air. Mountain snow sometimes falls in thick walls. Either way the air turns a milky white, the same milky white as the featureless, snow-covered ground, reducing visibility to zero. You lose the ability to tell earth from sky—and you are in a whiteout.

Snow can be an expectation or a surprise—in both cases you need to be prepared (NOLS).

Whiteouts occur where the terrain lacks trees or other vegetation. They are always terribly disorienting, and they can be dangerous: You cannot see a sudden drop-off in front of you or find your way to your intended destination. Here are some tips for handling a whiteout:

1. If you have a choice, choose to hunker down and wait it out.
2. If you have noted a major landmark prior to the whiteout—ridges, cliffs, trees, ravines—you might choose to head for it. If the swirling whiteness gives you brief glimpses of the landmark, you know you are on the right track.
3. If the sky seems to be building toward a whiteout, take a compass bearing on a landmark, and follow it.

Spring snow. The snow of spring, even when deep, can often be easily crossed on its frozen surface without snowshoes or skis if you travel early in the morning. When the sun softens the snow, you may end up postholing—breaking through the surface up to your knees or higher. If the sunny surface will not support you, try staying as much as possible in shade where the cold lingers longer. If you must posthole, keep your weight on your back leg, step halfway into your next footfall, and wait for the snow to firm up. If postholing overwhelms you, try crawling. In the high country, spring snowstorms often create dangerous avalanche conditions.

Glissading

One of the rewards of finding summer snowfields is the opportunity to do seated and standing glissades. For a seated glissade, sit on something slick and waterproof (such as a rain parka), point your feet downhill, and go. Use your heels to brake and steer. The standing glissade offers more control. Place your feet flat on the snow, one slightly behind the other. Flex your knees and bend forward at your waist. Use your boot edges to turn and stop. Check the runout before you start a glissade.

A seated glissade can be both a fun and a fast way to descend a snowy slope (NOLS/ Deborah Sussex).

Summer snow. The snow of summer is almost always old. Slopes covered in summer snow are most easily crossed in stiff-soled boots and a travel technique known as kick-stepping. Stand up straight to reduce the chance of slipping. Take short steps, and kick each booted foot firmly into the slope until you have a platform to stand on that is at least half the width of your boot. Step up onto the platform gently, pressuring your uphill boot edge. Then kick the next step. Summer snow can be marvelously slick. Always note the runout, the area you will slide into if you cannot arrest soon enough from a slip. If it looks dangerous, a cliff or a field of sharp rocks for instance, the wisest move is probably in another direction.

Fall snow. The snow of fall is usually a surprise, an early warning of the advance of winter. Problems presented by fall snow are typically associated more with routefinding than with actually hiking through the snow. Signs that the trail is under the snow include openings through the trees and breaks in the forest canopy overhead, subtle flattening across a hillside, sawed log ends, and blazes on trees. Stay tuned to your map.

Winter snow. The snow of winter is fresh and new, beautiful and sometimes dangerous. The danger arises primarily from avalanches. Knowledge of how to choose the best route through avalanche country is best gained in the company of others who already have the knowledge. For your routefinding ability to mature, you must travel many different types of terrain in many different types of weather. Safe routefinding is a combination of choices made before the trip starts as well as choices made during the trip.

Before heading into avalanche country, investigate the risk as completely as possible for that time of year. Some mountainous regions of the United States, and some in a few foreign countries, offer, as a public service, information and warnings about general avalanche danger. Specific information should be obtained from the nearest office of a government land management agency. If those offices

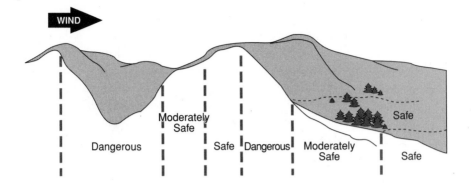

Choose a safe route to avoid an avalanche.

cannot help, and even if they can, more detailed info is often available from local ski areas, outdoor shops, newspapers, and radio stations.

The risk of an avalanche is usually rated as **low,** okay to go; **moderate,** go but be careful; **considerable,** somewhere between moderate and high, think about staying home, but if you go be *very* careful; **high,** not very smart to go without experience; and **extreme,** really stupid to go unless you are sure of a safe route. Remember, whatever the generally perceived risk of an avalanche, specific slopes may be ready to slide at any given moment, and a rating of low never eliminates the chance of an avalanche.

Safety in avalanche terrain can be summed up in five words: Stay away from dangerous areas. The most dangerous route of travel is one in which you may be the trigger for the avalanche. Stay off of avalanche release zones and stay out of avalanche paths. Stay off of leeward slopes and out from under cornices. Stay out of narrow ravines and slim valleys. Stay off of steep slopes, especially inclinations of 25–30 degrees or more, and very especially if the slope profile is convex. Thin stands of timber, where you can pass easily through, are thin enough for avalanches to pass easily through and should be avoided. Remember, during and immediately after a big storm, all mountainous areas should be considered unsafe, and the colder the temperature the longer the hazard will persist. Do not camp or even take rest breaks in an area of avalanche danger.

The safest route of travel is on top of ridges, and toward their windward side, above avalanche release zones. The second safest route is down the middle of wide valleys, away from deposition zones. Thick stands of timber usually offer a bothersome but safe route as well.

When your route will cross a slope that might avalanche, and you have thought it over and decided to give it a go, consider following this advice:

1. Think it over one more time. Is there an alternative route? If the slope does avalanche, what will the outcome be? Is it worth the risk? It is? Okay, then . . . .

2. Choose the safest route across the avalanche slope. Avoid the most likely trigger zones. Snow covers break off at points of greatest stress: near the top of a straight slope, at the steepest point of a convex slope, where an irregularity in the terrain (rocks, trees) breaks the snow surface. If the slope must be ascended or descended to gain the starting point of the safest route, go up or down on safe snow near the slope. If the dangerous slope itself must be ascended or descended to gain the safe starting point, follow the fall line instead of cutting across the fall line. This means go straight up or straight down the slope. If skis make this difficult, take them off and plow through the snow. If there are islands of safety on the slope, such as rock outcroppings or dense stands of timber, plan a route from one of these to the next. On an open slope, stay high where, at least, there is less snow to slide down from above.

3. Traverse the slope diagonally, from the top toward the bottom, not horizontally. Horizontal cuts tempt the snow to slide more than diagonal cuts. And try to avoid turns that take you back under an already potentially weakened slope. Ski turns especially add stress to the slope.

4. Loosen pack straps and undo hipbelts, unhitch safety straps on skis, loosen bindings on snowshoes and skis, and remove wrist loops on ski poles. Everything that an avalanche could catch and hold should be easy to shed. (Note: There is some evidence that a small, light pack may actually help you "float" on some avalanches.)

5. Tighten up clothing, put on a hat, pull up the parka's hood, slip on mittens. Once caught in an avalanche, snow that gets inside of clothing cools you faster, shortening your survival time.

6. If you have electronic rescue transceivers, make sure they are working, turned to transmit, secured somewhere on each person under at least one layer of clothing, and not in a pack that could be torn off.

7. Cross one at a time, after everyone is ready, with at least one person serving as a spotter at all times. The spotter can yell if an avalanche breaks loose, and watch the victim until he or she comes to rest or goes under. Generally, it is best for everyone to take the same trail across, but, with a large party, avoid following each other precisely, which cuts a deep trench through the snow, and may cut loose a slab. Do not stop until you have reached a safe spot.

8. Think it over one more time.

The Land of Very Up and Down

On very steep terrain, scrambling upward is safer and less awkward than climbing down. Your eyes are in the lead, making routes easier to follow and holds easier to find. And that explains, at least in part, why some people get stuck up high. They climb up steep slopes they later find too frightening or difficult to descend. If you are comfortable going up, and if you have no plan to return along the same

Steep terrain offers unique challenges (NOLS/Deborah Sussex).

route, keep going. But if you will need to climb down the same route you ascended, you are wise to look down while going up. If you do not think you can safely descend, find another way up.

When descending steep terrain that you feel unsafe standing on, face away from the slope and climb down crablike using your butt for friction. If the descent steepens even more, face sideways to the slope. This allows a good view of holds and the route below. When the route is nearly vertical, face directly into the cliff, as if you were climbing down a ladder.

Rockfall. On steep terrain beware the danger of falling rock. If possible, stay out of gullies, narrow passages that capture and direct falling rocks. Avoid entering or passing below a gully when sun is melting snow or ice, loosening the rocks above. If you do ascend or descend a gully, travel quickly, one at a time,

Tips from the Land of Up and Down

1. When hiking up steep terrain, loosen pack straps that inhibit your ability to twist and turn or step high. The stabilizer straps on the sides of your hipbelt are prime candidates for loosening, as are shoulder straps and load lifters.
2. When hiking downhill, pull your pack's hipbelt and stabilizer straps comfortably snug to prevent your load from shifting.
3. When hiking downhill, lace your boots snugly for optimal support and stability, and to avoid jamming your toes. But loosen the upper laces on tall, stiff boots so your ankle can flex fully forward and to relieve strain on your Achilles tendons.
4. Shorten trekking poles when hiking uphill, and lengthen them for descents. A "length" rule of thumb: Your elbow should be bent at about 90 degrees when you plant a pole. When ascending very steep terrain, or on sidehills, hold the uphill pole in the middle of the shaft so you do not need to make adjustments continually. Wrap strips of duct tape around the shaft for a better grip.
5. If you find yourself using handholds in the uphill battle, test every hold before you rely on it. Pull or kick down to see if it shifts. Listen for the sound it makes. A hollow "bonk" means the hold is loosely attached.

Tips for Crossing Steep Ice

▲ If you anticipate ice or hard snow on steep terrain, carry a lightweight ice axe and ultralight crampons.

▲ You can arrest a slide with an ice axe. The basics: Hold the head in one hand with your thumb under the adze and the pick end facing the snow. With your other hand, hold the shaft near the end. Press the pick into the snow by lying on the shaft as you hold it diagonally under your chest. At the same time, dig your toes into the snow (unless you are wearing crampons). Practice where there is a safe runout.

▲ You can self-belay with an ice axe. Hold the axe by its head in your uphill hand and walk with it like a cane. When the slope gets steep and you stop trusting your feet to maintain their grip, start pushing the shaft deeper into the snow. Stand with your uphill foot forward for better balance when you move the axe to its next placement. If you slip, plunge the shaft into the snow and hang on.

▲ If the surface is too hard to kick good steps (and you do not have crampons), cut foot holds with the adze end of the axe. Stand in the balanced position (uphill foot forward), hold the axe near its pike end, and swing with a straight arm. Try to cut two steps from one balance position, and then move into the new set of steps while using the axe in the self-belay position.

▲ Wearing crampons you can traverse a hard surface almost as easily as if the ground were bare. Key points to remember: Lift your legs slightly higher than normal so the points do not snag. Make sure your feet are flat against the snow so that all the points bite with each footfall. Prevent snow from "balling up" between crampon points by occasionally knocking your ice axe against the side of your foot. Always check and double-check bindings before putting yourself in the slide zone.

and do not climb directly above or below companions who could trigger the release of a stone shower. If staggered ascent is impossible, walk close together so rocks loosened by one hiker do not have time to gain speed before striking those below.

Talus. Large rocks piled onto and into a slope are called talus. Step directly on top of the rocks, moving slowly from one to another, always ready to hop to the next if the one you happen to land on shifts or rolls. If you can step on lichen-covered rocks without destroying the lichen, do so. Lichen is usually an indication that the rock has remained unmoved a long time.

Scree. Smaller rocks and loose dirt covering slopes are called scree. Soft scree is difficult—but not dangerous—to ascend but fun and easy to descend. Try kick stepping during the uphill battle and plunge stepping on the downhill romp, as you would on snow. For better traction going downhill on steep scree, zigzag with your feet angled across the slope rather than pointing straight down.

An ice axe can increase the fun and the safety of crossing steep snow or ice (NOLS/ Deborah Sussex).

The Land of Frozen Water

Glaciers. Glacier travel is hazardous because crevasses often lie hidden under snow. If falling into one does not kill you, they are almost always difficult to escape. Avoid crossing a glacier unless you are trained for crevasse rescue, have the appropriate gear, and can rope up with partners. The possible exception comes in late summer when snow has completely melted, making crevasses more obvious and easier to avoid. Without crampons, walk on the hardest, darkest ice, where grit and gravel provide traction.

Moraines. At the edges and toes of most glaciers are great piles of loose rock called moraines. Walk on these as you walk on talus, but remember that there may be slippery ice under the rocks, making them prone to sliding.

Frozen lakes. Traveling on flat frozen water can be a heck of a lot easier than wading through nearby snow—but it is not without hazards, even in northern climes where the ice may be several feet thick. Springs and swirling winds sometimes create thin ice, and danger, often difficult to detect until you plunge through. And snow-covered lakes may be covered with surprisingly thin ice because the snow could have insulated the surface of the water, preventing it from freezing solid enough to support you. If you are going to cross a frozen lake, keep these tips in mind:

▲ Wearing skis or snowshoes disperses your weight over a larger area, reducing the chance you will break through.

▲ Spots where streams enter and leave lakes are notorious for thin ice.

▲ Dark areas of ice are sometimes indicators of thin ice.

▲ Objects sticking out of the ice, such as logs and rocks, sometimes trap and radiate solar energy, creating weak spots.

▲ Tap the ice ahead of you with a trekking pole or stout stick. A solid thunk tells of thick ice, and a hollow bonk indicates thin ice.

▲ Sections of ice shadowed by trees or cliffs usually provide the thickest ice because the sun has less time to warm the area.

▲ If you fall through, do not panic. Spread your arms wide over the edge of the hole, and swim vigorously back up onto the ice.

Frozen rivers. Fast-moving water typically fails to freeze solid enough to support your weight, but slow-moving rivers may provide excellent pathways in the dead of winter. Pack the tips for crossing frozen lakes, and add these reminders:

▲ Avoid ice over the fastest current. Easily said, but not always easily done, the strongest current, and the weakest ice, tends to lie on the outside of bends and where the river drops.

▲ Wind-scoured ice tends to be weaker than the ice in sheltered areas.

▲ If you think the water is deep enough to submerse you, do not cross. A break-through can cause you to be sucked under the ice.

▲ Look for braids in the river where the flow separates into two or more narrower channels.

The Land of Running Water

Without bridge or stepping stones, the crossing of running water will vary from a simple wade in shallows to the challenge of waist-deep, ice-cold plunges.

Take these tips to heart:

- ▲ Scout downstream from your intended crossing point. If you do not think you can safely swim the downstream rapids or survive the drop over the waterfall, choose a different spot to cross.
- ▲ Before stepping too far from shore, assess the power of the flow. Calf-deep water can throw you face down when the current is strong. There will be safer spots to cross up or down the river. Look, for instance, for braided streambeds where big currents split into smaller, more manageable channels. Narrow flows may look quick, but a wide, smooth flow is usually easier to traverse. Beware the outside of a bend in a river where the current is typically deepest and strongest.
- ▲ A smooth flowing surface usually means the bottom of the river is relatively smooth. Cross there instead of where the surface is roiled by underlying rocks.
- ▲ High in the mountains, streams are typically easier to cross early in the morning before the sun melts the snowfields above and increases the flow.
- ▲ After a rainstorm, the water level will rise. Consider waiting for it to drop.
- ▲ Do not cross rivers barefooted. Wear your camp shoes, an old pair of running shoes, or your boots after removing your socks and boot insoles (so your boots will dry faster).
- ▲ Unbuckle your pack's hipbelt and sternum strap and loosen the shoulder straps so you can ditch the load quickly if the current sweeps you off your feet.
- ▲ Face upstream during the crossing. Your balance is better facing upstream, and you can keep a look out for debris floating downstream.
- ▲ The more legs the better, so use your trekking poles or a sturdy stick for balance. Probe ahead with the pole for unseen depths and rocks before taking the next step. In a group, hold hands or link arms for better balance.
- ▲ During a group crossing, send a strong person out first and place weaker hikers in the middle. Groups linked together, hand in hand, can cross side by side, but in strong currents the group can cross in tandem with the strongest hiker in front and the rest of the group spread out downstream. The stronger person blocks some of the current for weaker hikers.
- ▲ Avoid the deadly hazard of ankle entrapment by shuffling your feet instead of taking steps.
- ▲ In a very strong current, allow yourself to slip downstream diagonally instead of fighting straight across.
- ▲ Never, ever tie into a rope. If you slip, you can be dragged under the water.
- ▲ If you slip and cannot stand up immediately, ditch your pack and go swimming. Do not try to stand up. Your pack, in almost all cases, will float. Stay on your back with your feet pointed downstream to push off rocks. Swim for shore or quiet water.

Holding hands or linking arms crossing a river provides a group with stability and safety (NOLS/Tom Bol).

The Land of Never Winter

Few, if any, terrain features defy generalization more than deserts. Do you see, in your mind's eye, the limitless sandy swells of the Sahara Desert, the cacti blooming across the Sonoran Desert, the parched flats of the Great Basin, the tumbled stones of the Mojave—or perhaps the majestic sandstone immensity of the high desert of southern Utah. All deserts, however, demand a common offering on their bleached altars: Show your respect, or die. And here are several suggestions on how to show your respect:

▲ Learn as much as possible about the availability of water. But even so, you might find a spring that bubbled up for a thousand years is no longer bubbling. And natural tanks may

> **The Creek vs. the Brush**
>
> When the brush stands impenetrable but a stream runs through it, try walking in the water. Even thigh-deep water, not running too fast, can make for easier hiking than the neighboring jungle. But stay aware of waterfalls and tight canyons that do not have a safe exit.

be deceptively difficult to find. When water cannot be guaranteed, you are safest to suffer the burden of at least two gallons per person per day. At eight pounds per gallon, the desert trekker will not be able to plan much distance between short-term destinations—without a camel. Do not carry all your water in one container. If you spring a leak, you could be done for.

▲ Take preventative steps to avoid the illnesses and injuries associated with high heat and direct sunshine (see "Health and Safety," later in this section).

▲ Avoid most deserts in the summer. Spring and fall typically offer the most pleasant traveling conditions, although winters in some deserts can be very appealing.

▲ On a hot day, rise early and cover ground before making a midday stop in the shade. Nap away the most intense hours of sunlight. When afternoon shadows begin to lengthen, put in a few more miles.

▲ You may consider traveling at night, especially with a bright moon or a strong flashlight. But remember night is when the desert comes to life in the form of scorpions, snakes, and, in some areas, rather large lizards. And cacti are notoriously more difficult to dodge in the darkness.

The Land of Ebb and Flow

One of my first treks took me along 50 miles of wilderness beach, a stretch of sand and ragged rock accessed at only one point by a road. Exploring tide pools was an unending source of wonder. I never tired of watching seals watch me. I loved, and still love, the warmth of a driftwood fire below the high-tide mark, the smell of salty air, the eternal sound of lapping waves. If a quick check of your dream list does not reveal a beach trek, I highly recommend adding one. I can also recommend that you:

▲ **Carry a local tide table.** In addition to reading it and believing it you will also want to keep a wary eye on the tides near at foot. I wish to never again sit huddled on a wave-drenched rock waiting for the tide to go out and hoping that when it does I am still sitting huddled instead of being swept out to sea.

▲ **Prepare for diverse walking conditions.** Sand seems to make for slower going, whatever its density. Wading shoes seem a must for the unexpected (or expected) mudflat, river outlet, and unusually high tide.

▲ **Prepare for all kinds of weather and sudden changes in weather.** A hot, dry, still beach can turn cool, moist, and windy in a few heartbeats.

▲ **Camp well above the high-tide mark.** You never know when a rogue wave will disobey the rules.

▲ **Spend most of your time in the intertidal zone,** the area between low and high tides. The intertidal zone is very forgiving of trespass, but not so the fragile dunes and backshore regions.

Add a beach trek to your list of dreams.

Weather or Not

In terms of trekking, the rule with weather, as in most domains associated with the long trail, is Know Before You Go. Learn as much as possible, in other words, about what you can expect. And plan accordingly. Learn, more than anything else, the worst possible conditions you can expect. If it snowed and then froze hard there on a July day 100 years ago, it just might do it again while you are setting up camp. Underestimating the potential severity of the weather has destroyed more than one trekker.

Discuss the weather, whenever possible, with someone who has logged a lot of trail days in the area you intend to trek, and hear what they know about the climate of the region. Regions, especially anyplace with significant variations in elevation or with a large body of water nearby—such as an ocean or a really big lake—exhibit weather patterns that vary seasonally but are reasonably consistent from one year to the next. Spring winds, for instance, may blow prevailingly from one direction, helping you determine everything from choice of campsites to choice of routes. Daily high and low temperatures, as another example, may show huge swings or remain consistently within a narrow range. The bottom line: Knowing regional climate and weather patterns can be just as or even more useful to you as knowing a specific day's forecast.

Weather Forecast Tips

1. Television news or weather channels tend to focus on cities. Your destination may be experiencing very different weather. Remain aware of that fact.
2. If you have access to a radio station near your intended destination, you are more likely to get an accurate forecast (specific to your needs) than you will get from TV.
3. Newspapers will have some information about the forecast for the near future, but it may not meet your long-range needs.
4. The Internet provides a useful resource. Try the National Weather Service website (*www.nws.noaa.gov/*).
5. Federal land management agencies and regional backpacking clubs sometimes post the forecast outside a ranger station, visitor center, or office, or provide a phone number with a recording with the daily forecast.
6. Local knowledge is sometimes your best source of accurate and timely information about the weather. Nothing replaces someone who intimately knows the area you intend to travel.

Since the advice in the two paragraphs above only works if you read them before hitting the trail, hopefully you have done so. Once on the trail, the advice is simple: Pay attention (which, come to think of it, is sound advice in all areas of life). Even in weather that feels perfect, you want to remain keenly aware of what is happening in the sky and in the air. In the sky there are clouds, and in the air there are pressure changes and temperature changes—and they are constantly in touch with each other.

Tales the Sky Tells

Beyond all that weather information you have gathered lies the fact that the trail does not always listen to the forecast. Learn the forecast and the climate of the region, yes, but learn also to read the sky. You might not qualify for a job on the Five O'Clock News, but you can get advance warnings about weather changes and walk more wisely into that land beyond the thermostat.

▲ **High, wispy cirrus clouds**—the mare's tails of common parlance—are made of ice crystals and herald the arrival of rain or snow, or at least some change in the weather, within 24 hours or so.

Cirrus clouds (Jeff Renner)

A lenticular cloud (Jeff Renner)

Fast-moving clouds may announce a change in the weather (Jeff Renner).

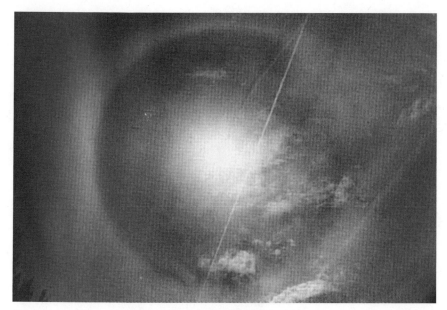

A halo around the sun may forecast precipitation (Jeff Renner).

- ▲ **A lenticular cloud**—the cap of cloud that forms like a giant upside-down bowl above a peak—tells you a mountain's upper elevations are getting hammered by very strong winds. It also warns that precipitation is likely to follow within 48 hours.
- ▲ **Puffy white cumulus clouds** may bring nothing more than some wind and an opportunity to find pictures in the sky. But if they thicken, tower upward, and darken into cumulonimbus clouds, a storm is building.
- ▲ **Low and fast-moving clouds** are usually accompanied by strong wind, and may signal a coming change in the weather: a storm could be building or a storm could be leaving.
- ▲ **A wide ring, or halo,** surrounding the moon by night or the sun by day often means precipitation will begin within a day or two. If the ring is narrow and tight, the precip might be no more than 12 hours away.

Tales the Air Tells

Barometric pressure. Air pressure is the weight of the atmosphere pressing down on the surface of our planet. It can be measured, just in case you are interested, by a barometer in units called millibars. In nice weather, the barometer rarely drops much below 30. A high-pressure system means heavier air, and that usually brings cooler temperatures and clear skies. A low-pressure system brings the opposite: warmer temps and the resulting storms. Air pressure decreases as you gain altitude because there are fewer air molecules overhead.

Weather Safety Tips

▲ Always be prepared for the worst possible weather you can expect.

▲ Monitor the sky and the air for changes at all times, especially when you are above the relative protection of tree line.

▲ Be conscious of escape routes from high country in case a storm roars in without due warning.

▲ Make sure all members of your party know the inclement weather plan.

▲ Enjoy the journey instead of being overly focused on the day's destination. Accept the fact that the weather might call for a change of plans.

If you have a barometer, and the air pressure starts to drop, it means clouds are going to build and precipitation is going to fall. A rise in the numbers on the barometer usually indicates the opposite: clearing skies. It is unlikely that you will have a barometer, but an altimeter can sometimes serve if you remember to think in reverse. Although altimeters are affected by other factors, such as heat, one that tells you the altitude is rising—when you are not—tells you the barometer is falling, and thus a storm front lies just over the horizon. The altimeter that falls when you do not tells you of clearing skies. Some people claim they can feel the pressure changes, especially a drop in pressure, in their old joints. I never argue with these people.

Temperature. In addition to air pressure, the temperature of the air has tales to tell—or demands to make. Many of the challenges you will face trekking arise from the air temperature, and the fact that it walks hand in weathered hand with wind and other changes in the immediate environmental conditions. Temperature, for instance, can alter the surface of the ground—from, say, firm to muddy—and change the speed at which you travel. Temperature affects what you wear, where you camp, how much you eat, and how you feel. From ambient air temperature comes the risk of some illnesses and injuries (see "Health and Safety," later in this section).

If the day brings no big changes in weather, the air will warm slowly, generally speaking, throughout the hours of sunshine. Shortly after sundown, the temperature will start to drop, reaching its low point just before sunrise. In some regions, however, temperature changes during the day are vast. A desert, for instance, can go from a chilly early morning to a burning late evening—and that is normal. Also keep in mind that the temperature drops as you gain altitude, another normal phenomenon.

But when you notice the air suddenly warming, a warm front (a warm mass of air) is moving in. A warm front drifts in above the colder air that is already there, forming thin clouds. The cold air below is slowly moving out. If the warm air rises fast enough, the clouds may thicken and drop rain. If the temperature suddenly drops, a cold front (a cold air mass) is bullying its way in below the warmer air already there. A cold front tends to cause a quick rise in warmer air, which tends to form clouds heavy with moisture, and precipitation falls. Cold fronts, therefore, are more often associated with rapid weather changes and more dramatic storms. A thermometer is helpful here, but not necessary if you are paying attention.

Weather Happens

Wind. Residents of a tropical rainforest might argue, but for most of us wind is the most persistent and consistent disturbance on the trail related to weather. Wind, on the plus side, can blow away pestiferous insects. On the other side of the windscreen, moving air tends to detract from your stove's ability to function. It can turn a pleasant day unpleasant, or even dangerous by tearing away body heat or ripping limbs off overhanging trees. Even beneath modern, wind-shedding clothing, wind can steal energy.

Wind can be prevailing and/or determined by topography. Prevailing winds,

Understanding Wind Chill

When the wind blows, the cold feels colder. The stronger the wind blows, the colder you feel. Most people understand this. Many people, however, are not aware of the fact that the temperature of the air, whether it is moving or not, is the same. You feel colder because moving air sucks out heat faster than still air. If the thermometer reads 40 degrees F, it will read the same no matter how fast the wind blows. Your skin cannot drop below 40 degrees (with a couple of exceptions such as skin that is wet with white gas). But the wind will drop your skin's temperature faster—and so you feel colder—and, if the temperature is low enough for your skin to freeze (frostbite), it will freeze faster in wind.

The wind chill index is an indicator of how fast your exposed skin cools off at a given air temperature when the wind is blowing at a given speed. The old wind chill index, in effect for many years, was replaced in 2000 by a new index that gives much more realistic values. The new wind chill index also covers a wider range of temperatures (from 40 degrees F to minus 35 degrees F) and wind speeds (from 3 to 60 miles per hour). As a sample, the new index tells you that an air temperature of 5 degrees F and a wind speed of 25 miles per hour chills your skin as fast as a still air temperature of minus 17 degrees F. The new chart also provides a calculation of how fast frostbite can occur on exposed skin at wind chill temperatures across the chart. (See Appendix A.)

Windy Facts

▲ Polar winds tend to blow east to west.

▲ Middle latitude winds, those crossing the United States, tend to blow west to east.

▲ Tropic winds tend to blow east to west.

▲ In the mountains, early morning wind tends to push downslope from cooler temperatures up high. As the day warms and air rises, winds tend to blow upslope.

▲ Since water cools and warms slower than land masses, ocean winds tend to blow onshore (toward land) during the day, from cooler water to warmer land. During the night, ocean winds tend to blow offshore (toward water), from cooler land to warmer water.

▲ High cliffs and dense tree cover can swirl winds all about, giving you little chance to guess where they will come from.

as the term implies, are those air movements that are consistent in a given area in a given season. Some winds can be remarkably predictable in direction, strength, and timing. When wind slams up against a mountain or ridge, the moving air is forced to flow up and over the land. This "orographic effect" funnels a lot of wind through the first break in the topography of the land—say, a mountain pass—or up and over a summit. This phenomenon explains why the wind may blow through mountain passes, on summits, and along the crest of a ridge, with considerably more ferocity than wind even a short distance below the summit or off the ridge. By studying a topographical map of your intended journey, you can see where you are likely to encounter the worst winds—the passes, summits, and ridge crests as well as the windward slopes and the high plateaus on the leeward side of passes. Remember: Predicted winds and their speed relate to a general area, and you will find great variability depending on where the topography concentrates the wind. This kind of information can help you decide where to hike as well as to anticipate ahead of time the clothing you want to keep handy in case the wind arises. A wise trekker learns the habits of local winds.

Rain. At any given time, the atmosphere of the earth holds an estimated 3100 cubic miles of water in the form of vapor, clouds, and precipitation. When the water falls, it can come down, as you know, in anything from a fine fog to a flood, in anything from warm vapor to ice-laden chunks. In all forms, rain complicates life on the trail.

Fog is formed by tiny droplets of water floating in the air—not quite rain, but far from dry. Visibility can be obscured, sometimes remarkably, and you can end up as wet as from a light rain. In cold temperatures, fog can put a layer of ice on the ground without precipitation actually occurring. (The technical term for this change of water vapor in the air directly into ice—or, vice versa, the conversion of ice directly into water vapor—is sublimation.)

A **freezing rain** is one that turns to ice when it contacts any surface cold enough to make ice. It can turn your traveling surface into a hockey rink. **Sleet** is made of frozen raindrops (or sometimes snow that has melted and refrozen). Pellets of sleet, covering the ground like little ball bearings, can make travel even more treacherous than freezing rain.

In the absence of an up-to-the-minute forecast, you can guess when precipitation will fall, even though you may not be able to guess in what form. But whether it falls or not you should have a watertight plan for rainy days. Here are some thoughts on waterproofing your camp:

▲ When you anticipate quite a bit of rain on your trek, consider carrying a tarp as a supplemental shelter. Ultralight models are available. A tarp can serve as a separate roof or as an extension to your tent's vestibule.

▲ Consider carrying a tent with a spacious vestibule, where you can store wet gear, keep gear dry, or even cook dinner with the door open for ventilation.

▲ If you have to set up your tent during a downpour, remember that tents with poles that slip through sleeves usually pitch faster than those that attach with clips.

▲ If your tent has a mesh ceiling, consider another tent. Condensation that forms on the inside of the rainfly can and will drip through the mesh.

▲ Make sure you have seam-sealed every stitch that does not have a factory seal. Seal your tent before leaving home. You do not need to carry the extra weight, and the sealer requires about 24 hours of drying.

▲ A well-ventilated tent prevents much of the condensation that accompanies rain from forming. Keep doors at least partially open and vents open.

▲ Keep your tent set taut. Tighten the rainfly straps and guylines to keep the fly and tent walls separated. This improves air circulation and reduces condensation.

▲ In rainy climes, choose a synthetic sleeping bag. It soaks up less water and dries faster than a down bag.

▲ Keep your sleeping bag and clothing away from the entrance, and avoid contact with wet floors and walls. Keep your spare clothing, and anything else you want to keep dry, inside waterproof stuff sacks or plastic bags.

▲ Avoid pitching your tent in a depression. Even if you see no water collected there, it could collect later. Good tent floors will not let water in, but rain will puddle under your vestibule.

▲ Some tents come with integral clotheslines—a good thing. If your tent does not have one, tie a line across the tent ceiling to dry wet clothes and gear.

Thunderstorms. The discomfort of thunderstorms comes from wind and wet. The danger comes from lightning. The danger of the awesome and unpredictable power of lightning cannot be overemphasized. To maximize your safety, follow these guidelines:

1. Know local weather patterns. Lightning storms, in general, tend to roll in quickly on summer afternoons. Do not be out in the open and/or above tree line. Refrain from being anywhere near the highest point around.
2. Plot storms. When the flash of lightning precedes the boom of thunder by five seconds, the storm is approximately 1 mile away—if you matched the flash and boom correctly. To be the safest, find a safe spot, and stay put when the storm, and the lightning, is 5–6 miles away.
3. Find a safe spot. Avoid high places, high objects, metal objects, open places, open bodies of water, and long conductors such as fences. Seek uniform cover such as the lowest spot in low rolling hills or a stand of trees of all about the same size (but avoid touching any tree). Deep dry caves are usually safe. If you happen to still be in your vehicle, stay in it with the windows rolled up.
4. Assume a safe position when outdoors. Squat or sit in a tight position on insulating material. Spread groups out, but try to keep everyone in sight.

Campsite Selection

Back when there were more trees to camp beneath and less people to camp away from, the late and incomparably great Paul Petzoldt, founder of NOLS, coached his students to select a campsite with consideration for the Four W's: Weather, Widowmakers, Water, and Wood. Great advice stands up to the test of time and, with the elaboration on the meaning of the W's that follows, you still hear the ring of truth in Paul's words.

With the sun low, half hidden behind a tree-lined ridge to the west, and daylight fading fast, you have already failed to follow the prime directive in campsite selection: Do not wait until daylight is fading fast to select a campsite. As Paul wrote, "Few persons can make camp after dark without danger of fatigue, irritability, accidents, or environmental damage." A wise trekker plans the day in order to arrive with the sun still providing adequate illumination. If the trail runs longer than you suspected and the day draws toward a close before you planned, wisdom would further dictate that you stop as soon as you find a likely spot instead of pushing on into the night. In this case, if you cannot see, you cannot do.

Okay, you have plenty of light, so what do you want to do with it? You want to look for, foremost, a site free of threats to the well-being of yourself and those with you. If Weather threatens with a chance of lightning, do not set camp in the open or on ridges where you could be a primary target, or near tall trees where you could be a secondary target (see "Weather or Not," above).

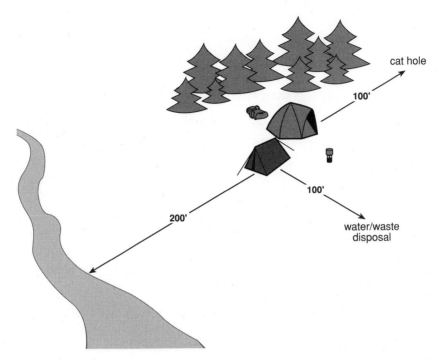

cat hole

100'

100'

200'

water/waste
disposal

Proper campsite selection protects you and the environment.

Look down. If you see evidence rain has puddled or run through your choice of campsites, choose another site with more elevation. More than a discomfort in canyon country, dry washes can become raging torrents of water within minutes when rain falls.

Look up. "Widowmakers" are large, dead limbs that could fall. Stay out from underneath those limbs, and from underneath dead trees that could topple in a high wind. Set camp away from the edge of cliffs that someone might stumble off or the bottom of cliffs that rocks could tumble onto. When snow covers the ground, camp away from the bottom of slopes down which avalanches could slide. On beaches, camp above the high tide mark.

All trekkers need Water, and great campsite selection includes a nearby source of that sweet, clear fluid. Avoidance of adding human pollution to natural water sources, however, should rank high on your priority list. Set your kitchen and your tent at least 200 feet, about 70 adult paces, from springs, streams, rivers, ponds, and lakes (see "Leave No Trace," earlier in this section). In some areas, out of a desperate need to preserve water quality—and the overall quality of the wilderness experience—land managers have established regulations that demand you set camp an acceptable distance from sources of water.

Now you can start thinking about your comfort. In addition to flat ground, search for a site that will drain well if rain falls. Gravel, sand, and deep forest debris all drain well. Compressed soil and ground already soggy obviously do not. Digging trenches to divert rainfall is a no-no. Lie down on the ground. If you detect a tilt to your bedroom floor, make sure you orient your shelter to keep your head higher than your feet. Lying down first also allows you to find hidden roots and rocks buried beneath those soft-looking leaves. If surface rocks or downed limbs compete for the otherwise perfect sleeping place, move them, but please replace them before you leave if moving them left scars. The next camper does not want to look at scars you have left and will not be encouraged to camp in exactly the same place.

Wind can be a blessing and a curse. Breezes can drive away obnoxious insects, adding much to the serenity of a tent site. Gusty winds can keep you awake by "rattling the walls" and threatening to turn your tent or tarp into a kite. If wind poses a problem, choose a site behind natural windbreaks: a thick stand of trees, large rocks, or a rise in the ground. Pitch your sleeping quarters with the low end toward the wind, and pitch it as tight as possible.

If it feels like a cold night lies ahead, chose a site that is high rather than low. Cold air sinks keeping the upper end of a valley slightly warmer than the lower end. Select a site, if you can, that will catch the early morning sun, adding many degrees to the joy of your own rising.

If you think your tent site causes the greatest harm to the environment, you think wrong. It is your kitchen. Where the group gathers, where most of the standing, sitting, shuffling, shifting, and stomping takes place is where you cook. Build a fire (the Wood of Paul Petzoldt's Four W's admonition) and, of course, the impact reaches all time heights. If your cooking requires only a stove—as it should—

set it on a flat rock or sandy soil if possible. Once again, dry grassy spots or the natural litter of a forest floor serve as second best high-use sites. This could mean your kitchen lies a walk of a couple of minutes away from your tent. So what. Vary the path you walk back and forth between tent and stove to prevent the creation of an impromptu trail.

Curious? Hungry? Disturbed? Black bears are best avoided no matter their mood (Alan Bauer).

The Bear Facts

▲ If there exists an Ursine Camping Rule Number One, it is this: Do not camp in places bears like. If you see scat, bear tracks, claw marks on trees, juicy berries, salmon leaping upstream, gnawed carcasses, or bears, keep on hiking.

▲ In country heavy with bears, look for a tent site out in the open. Bears will see you a long way off and you will see bears, maybe, a long way off. Bears do not like surprises.

▲ Feel free to make a reasonable amount of noise while camping in bear country.

▲ Your trash may be bear treasure. Practice clean camping. Consider all garbage attractive and keep it separately bagged within your food bag. If you burn garbage, consign it to the flames early in the day and bag anything that remains unburned.

▲ Cache all food and anything else fragrant, such as toothpaste, soap, chewing gum, chewing tobacco. You have three choices. You can hang your food bag in a tree. If money abounds and weight is not a problem, you can store food in a bear-proof container. When trees are scarce, double bag your food in plastic and store it on the ground at least 300 feet from your tent.

Store food out of reach.

Health and Safety

This information in no way intends or pretends to be a substitute for wilderness medical training. Such training is highly recommended and available from several reliable sources (see Appendix A).

"Words can describe a glass of water, but they cannot quench your thirst."
Zen saying

Hydration

If you are not drinking enough water to maintain a healthy fluid balance, you can alter, and even harm, every physiological function of your body. The water in your body, the fluid that keeps you alive and trekking, leaves you at an alarming rate. An average person on a normal day loses 3 to 6 liters of water. One to two liters rush out as urine in a well-hydrated person, and another $\frac{1}{10}$ liter in defecation. Moisture lost from the act of breathing may fill one to two 1-liter water bottles a day, depending on your level of exertion and the dryness of the air. And then there is sweat. Your perspiration totals 1–2 liters on an average day, but that amount can climb to 1–2 liters per hour during periods of hard exercise.

How can you tell you are running low on water? At first the signs are subtle. Your urine turns light yellow. You will get a mild headache, and then start feeling tired. When your body uses merely a liter and a half, your endurance may be reduced 22 percent and your maximum oxygen uptake (a measure of heart and lung efficiency) can be lowered 10 percent. And your thirst mechanism, that feeling of "Gosh, I need a drink," does not kick in until you are about a liter and half low. Down 3–4 liters can leave your endurance decreased to 50 percent and your oxygen uptake reduced close to 25 percent. By now, if you are observant, you will have noticed your urine has turned a dark yellow. You may suddenly find yourself seriously dehydrated: disoriented, irritable, heart pounding, completely pooped.

So, what is a body to do? Drink, of course, is the answer—but what, how much, and when? Unfortunately, some of the answers remain controversial. You can, despite the controversy, get by on plain water. Since internal water is used faster than the need for replenishment is felt, water should be consumed at a disciplined rate. There is considerable benefit from starting each day drinking a large volume of water, about half a liter. Following that, the Sports Medicine Institute International recommends ½–⅔ ounce of water

Gone are the days when you could safely take water directly from a stream (NOLS/ Deborah Sussex).

per pound of body weight per day, ingested periodically throughout the day. Figured in liters, you should drink about 3–4 liters per day for the average-sized person on the average trail. Drink water with meals and snacks, to encourage digestion, and suck down a few swallows before bedtime to replace what you will lose in sleep.

When hiking under a heavy pack, you should be pounding down water on a more disciplined schedule. Since the human body can only absorb so much water at one time, the rate of ingestion should be matched, as closely as possible, to the rate of absorption. Most of us have been classified for years into a rate-of-absorption range of ¼ liter per fifteen minutes. Recent research indicates some of us can do better, absorbing as much as ¼ liter in ten minutes. That means, for maximum efficiency and well-being, drink about ¼ liter of water every ten to fifteen minutes during periods of intense exercise. In some conditions you will lose water faster than you can replace it. In those conditions, rest breaks, during which fluid is consumed, become important.

In the end, for wilderness travel, and for life in general, the old piece of advice to drink enough water to keep your urine clear and copious rings with truth in most cases. But, yes, you can drink too much water (see the "Hyponatremia" sidebar).

Good Water vs. Bad Water

Gone are the days when you could throw yourself down on your belly, tired and thirsty, and slurp up water from a crystalline stream. It might be good—and it might be bad. And the only safe bet is to disinfect wilderness water before drinking.

Boiling. By the time water has reached the boiling point, even at high altitudes, the organisms that cause disease are dead. The water does not have to roll around like a sea in a perfect storm to be safe to drink.

Filters. Some filters strain out only protozoa, such as *Giardia* and *Cryptosporidium*. Some filter out protozoa and bacteria. None filter out viruses, but some have an iodine-resin on the filter that may kill viruses. In most of the wildland of the United States, waterborne viruses are not a problem. Outside the United States,

---

Substitutes for Plain Water

1. Coffee: Approximately half the coffee you drink counts as water.
2. Soda: Approximately half the soda you drink counts as water.
3. Milk, soy milk: Counts the same as water but requires more digestion.
4. Fruit juices: Count the same as water but with a high caloric content.
5. Herbal teas: Count the same as water.
6. Caffeinated teas: Approximately two-thirds of the tea you drink counts as water.
7. Alcoholic beverages: Not a good substitute for water, and actually dehydrate you.

All water should be disinfected either by filtering, boiling, or halogenating (NOLS/Deborah Sussex).

you definitely want a filter that gets rid of as many viruses as possible. Read the package carefully.

Chemicals. Called halogens, some chemicals are very good at killing everything harmful in water. Iodine and chlorine are the safest and most effective, but no chemical guarantees water safe from *Cryptosporidium*. A halogen can be added to water after using a filter that removes only protozoa to guarantee safe water. In most cases, iodine is the preferred chemical because it stores better and reacts less with organic compounds in water. Iodine is commercially available in several forms including tablets and crystals. Follow the directions on the label.

Common Injuries

The longer the trek, the greater the chance your trekking machine, the human body, is going to require some repair work.

Wounds

When an open wound is the problem, three goals are worthy of consideration: stop serious bleeding, prevent infection, and promote healing.

Bleeding. Almost all bleeding can be stopped with direct pressure and elevation: Pressure from your hand directly on the wound and elevation of the wound above the bleeder's heart. With enough time, place a sterile dressing on the wound before applying pressure. When immediate action is critical, grab anything absorbent to press into the wound. Keep in mind you can let small wounds bleed to a stop, a process that may actually clean them a bit.

Wound cleaning. Proper wound cleaning, closing, and dressing will represent the prevention of infection in most wounds. Cleaning also speeds healing and reduces scarring. The best method for cleaning is mechanical irrigation. Irrigation involves a high-pressure stream—preferably from an irrigation syringe—of an acceptable solution directed into the wound. The best cleaning solution is plain disinfected water. Draw the solution into the syringe, hold it 2 to 4 inches above the wound and perpendicular to the wound, and push down forcefully on the plunger. Keep the wound tipped so the solution runs out. Use at least half a liter, more if the wound still looks unclean. Without an irrigation syringe, you can improvise by using a biking water bottle, melting a pinhole in the center of the lid of a standard water bottle, or punching a pinhole in a clean plastic bag.

Wound closure. After thoroughly cleaning small wounds that gape open, facial wounds, or scalp wounds, close them with closure strips or strips of tape to promote healing. If you had to hold a wound open to thoroughly irrigate it, the wound should probably be taped shut. If hair gets in the way, it can be carefully clipped short, but avoid shaving away hair. If you have tincture of benzoin compound, smear a line along both sides of the wound; however, benzoin is an irritant so take care to keep it out of the wound. Let the benzoin dry for about 30 seconds. Benzoin's stickiness will help keep the closure strips in place. Take time to carefully tape the skin back exactly in its natural position.

Dressing and bandaging. The primary covering of a wound is the dressing. Sterile, non-adherent, porous, resistant to bacterial invasion, and easy to use dressings are the best. Wounds heal faster with less scarring if they are kept slightly moist with an antibiotic ointment or with a dressing that holds in the body's moisture while keeping out external moisture. The dressing should completely cover the wound and ideally extend a half-inch or so beyond the wound's edge. You will not have the ideal dressing unless you pack it in a first-aid kit, but you can improvise by boiling strips of cloth, such as a tee shirt cut into strips, and allowing them to dry before use.

The function of the bandage is to fix, protect, and further assist the dressing. It can be conforming gauze, tape, elastic wraps, clean cotton strips, or anything available. For very small wounds, the dressing and the bandage are available as a unit, as with the common adhesive strip bandages found in all first-aid kits.

Wound infection. Check all wounds regularly for signs of infection: increasing pain, heat, redness, and swelling; pus; appearance of red streaks just under the skin near the wound; and systemic fever. At the first signs of infection, reopen the wound, and let it drain. You may need to encourage the process by soaking the wound in hot water. Pack the wound with moist, sterile gauze to keep it draining, and dress it with dry, sterile gauze. Wet-to-dry dressings encourage draining. Re-clean and repack the wound twice a day, if possible.

Burns

First and foremost, stop the burning process—and the faster the better. Burns can continue to cause harm long after the flames are out. Cool the burn with water until the pain is gone. Do not try to remove hot plastic or anything else melted into the burn. Then follow these general guidelines:

1. Gently wash the burn with soap and water. Pat dry.
2. Remove the skin from blisters that have popped open—but do not open closed blisters.
3. Dress the burn with a thin layer of antibiotic ointment.
4. Cover the burn with a gauze pad, a layer of roll gauze, or clean clothing.
5. If you have no ointment, no dressings, or no skill, leave the burn alone. The burn's surface will dry into a scablike covering that provides a significant amount of protection.

Strains, Sprains, and Fractures

Strains. Over-stretching a muscle and/or the tendons that attach muscles to bones causes a strain. Strains can range from a mild annoyance to debilitating. A strained muscle or tendon can be used within the limits of pain—in other words, if it hurts, stop using it. RICE (Rest, Ice, Compression, and Elevation) can be helpful.

Blisters

Blisters, the most common problem faced by long-distance trekkers, are mild burns caused by friction. Friction produces a separation of the tough outer layer of skin from the sensitive inner layer. Blisters form only where your skin is thick and hard enough for this to happen. Loose skin just wears away with friction, leaving an abrasion. Blisters range from unpleasant to terribly debilitating. But they are not a serious problem unless they become infected.

Once the bubble develops, draining is far better than having a blister rupture inside a dirty sock. Clean around the site thoroughly. Sterilize the point of a needle or knife, and gently open the blister. Massage the fluid out. Leaving the roof of the blister intact will make it feel better and heal faster. If the roof has been rubbed away, treat the wound as you would any other, but include a dressing that limits friction, such as a piece of moleskin with a hole cut in the center. Fill the hole with a lubricating ointment. A piece of tape or moleskin over the hole will keep the ointment in place.

Blisters can be prevented by wearing boots or shoes that fit and are broken in, wearing a thin inner sock under a thicker outer sock, treating "hot spots" with a protective covering before the bubble forms, and taking off your boots to let your feet dry when you take a break from hiking.

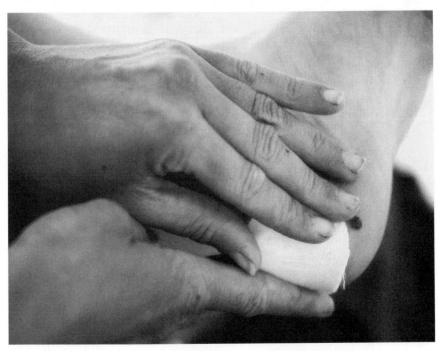

Blisters are the most common source of trail discomfort (NOLS/Deborah Sussex).

Sprains. Sprains are injuries to ligaments, the bands holding bones to bones at joints. The injury can vary from small to very large. Sensible action, in all cases, requires adequate first aid. First aid in this case is HIRICE: Hydration, Ibuprofen, Rest, Ice, Compression, and Elevation. Do not use the injury (Rest) for the first half hour or so while you reduce its temperature (Ice) as much as possible without freezing. Without ice, soak the joint in cold water, or carry chemical cold packs, or wrap the joint in wet cotton and let evaporation cool the damaged area. Compression requires an elastic wrap. Wrap it snug but not tight enough to cut off healthy circulation. Elevation refers to keeping the injury higher than your heart—if you are the injured person, of course. After twenty to thirty minutes of RICE, remove the treatment and let the joint warm naturally for ten to fifteen minutes before use. (Note: The injury will heal faster if RICE is repeated often until pain and swelling subside.) Stay well hydrated, and, if possible, following the directions on the label, continue taking ibuprofen for up to two weeks. If the injury remains unusable, you will have to build a splint and find a physician.

Fractures. Broken bones are sometimes simple to assess. Bones stick out through the skin, or joints are created where no joint should exist. Without the obvious, and without an x-ray, you can base an assessment on whether or not the injured area is useable. If it cannot be used, it is treated as if it is fractured. When in doubt, splint.

A splint should immobilize the broken bone(s), prevent further injury, and maximize comfort until a medical facility can be reached. To do this best, a splint needs to be made of something to pad the injury comfortably and something rigid enough to provide support. Padding should fill all the spaces within the system to prevent movement of the injury. In addition, a splint should be long enough to immobilize the joints above and below a broken bone, or immobilize the bones above and below an injured joint. Splints should immobilize the injury in the position of function, or as close to position of function as possible.

Only your imagination limits your choice of splinting materials: sleeping bags, foamlite pads (they can be cut to fit the problem), extra clothing, soft debris from the forest floor stuffed into extra clothing. For rigidity there are items such as sticks, tent poles, ski poles, ice axes, portable camp chairs, and internal and external pack frames. Splints can be secured in place with things like bandannas, strips of clothing, pack straps, belts, and rope. Useful items in your first-aid kit for securing splints include tape, elastic wraps, and roll gauze.

Common Illnesses

It is a microscopic jungle out there—viruses, bacteria, protozoa—and many of the invisible life-forms are not only looking for a host but also would find you a delightful place of residence.

Diarrhea

The backcountry is home to a multitude of diarrhea-causing germs. They will produce, generally speaking, one of two kinds of diarrhea:

Noninvasive diarrhea. Microbial colonies develop on upper small intestine walls with noninvasive diarrhea, leading to abdominal cramping, nausea, vomiting, and massive amounts of water, filled with salt and potassium, rushing out of your bowels.

Invasive diarrhea. Sometimes called dysentery, invasive diarrhea develops in the lower intestine and colon, with bacteria causing inflammation, bloody bowel movements, fever, abdominal cramping, and painful release of loose stools.

> ### Complicated Fractures
>
> When you see angles in bones in the wrong place, realignment to normal anatomical position is recommended. Pull gentle traction on the broken bone along the line in which it lies. This relaxes the muscles and reduces the pain allowing you to move the broken bone slowly and gently back into normal alignment. The sooner this movement takes place the better. Do not use force. Do not continue until you get complaints of increasing pain. Once aligned, splint as usual. If alignment cannot be achieved, splint as best you can.
>
> An open wound over a fracture, with or without visible bones, requires aggressive irrigation and dressing of the wound prior to splinting. If bone ends stick out of the wound, and if the doctor is more than 4–6 hours away: clean the wound and bone ends with irrigation, apply gentle traction-in-line to the fracture and pull the bone ends back under the skin, dress the wound, and splint. Infection is on the way, but bones live longer inside the body.

> ### Rib Fractures
>
> Broken ribs can be protected by supporting the arm on the injured side and securing it to the body. Regular deep breaths, even if it hurts, should be encouraged to keep the lungs clear. Be sure to watch for increasing difficulty breathing, an indication of a punctured lung—a physician should be found soon.

Whatever the cause, dehydration is the immediate problem with diarrhea. Mild diarrhea can be treated with water or diluted fruit juices or sports drinks. Persistent diarrhea requires more aggressive replacement of electrolytes lost in the stool. Oral rehydration solutions are best for treating serious diarrhea. You can get by, usually, adding one teaspoon of salt and eight teaspoons of sugar to a liter of water. The sufferer should drink about a quarter of this solution every hour, along with all the water he or she will tolerate. Bland food such as rice, grains, bananas, and potatoes are okay to eat. Fats, dairy products, caffeine, and alcohol should be avoided. Antidiarrheal drugs should be considered for your first-aid kit (see "Health and Safety" in Before You Go). If the diarrhea is not under control in 24–72 hours, the best trail leads to a doctor.

Upper Respiratory Infections

Colds. Those illnesses we call "colds" are often viral infections of the nasal passages and throat that cause a runny nose, sore throat, coughing, sneezing, headache, mild fever, muscle aches, and a general feeling of "I want my mommy." The illness may last from several days to several weeks. In the meantime, you can offer treatment by encouraging rest and hydration and suggesting ibuprofen for the discomfort of aches and pains and a decongestant for stuffiness. Your treatment

Dental Emergencies

Pain usually heralds the appearance of a tooth problem, and teeth annually account for a surprisingly large number of reasons that trekkers come home earlier than planned.

Cavities. The pain occurs when cold, food, or your tongue hit the spot. After rinsing the area clean, a drop of oil of cloves (eugenol) will ease the pain. Temporary fillings are the treatment of choice, and products are available for your first-aid kit. To improvise, fill the cavity with candle wax, ski wax, or sugarless gum. Temporary filling material can also be used to hold a dislodged crown in place.

Tooth knocked out. If a tooth is knocked out, there is a small chance it can be salvaged if you can get it back in the hole it used to live in. After rinsing the tooth off (do not scrub it), press it gently back in. If it will not go back in, at least save it until you find a dentist. And the same can be said for a piece of tooth that has broken off.

Exposed pulp. When a broken tooth exposes the pulp, pain can be extreme. A small piece of aspirin placed directly and carefully on the exposed pulp causes a burning pain, but it cauterizes the pulp, putting an end to your distress—at least for a while.

Infected tooth. A lot of swelling in the gum and cheek near the tooth usually indicates an infection. Discoloration may be visible. You need a dentist as soon as possible to have the abscess drained and antibiotics started. Cold packs on the cheek may give some temporary relief.

Pre-trip tips. Consult your dentist at least one month prior to a trek in order to have potential problems identified and treated. Routine oral hygiene will prevent most trek-ruining dental problems: floss once a day, and brush twice a day with a soft-bristled toothbrush.

addresses the symptoms and not the cause, but, in most cases, the illness will self-limit. The challenge, medically speaking, is to recognize when a mild illness is turning into a more serious illness.

Flu. A flu is medically distinct from the common cold. Although the signs and symptoms may be similar to a cold, a flu typically comes on more abruptly with more of an impact on the sufferer. Unfortunately, there is nothing more, treatment-wise, you can do in the field for the flu-ridden than you can do for the cold-ridden. Flus will usually self-limit as well. Bad things you need to watch for include: sudden worsening, high fever, difficulty breathing, unmanageable vomiting or diarrhea, and/or a cough that produces nasty sputum. If the illness comes on suddenly, fails to respond to treatment within 24 hours, or develops some of the characteristics of bad things, you need a doctor.

Environmental Hazards

Although you might say, and reasonably so, that the "environment" is a large part of what attracted you to the trek, that same environment—with its cold or heat, intense sunlight or high altitude—can also challenge your body.

Hypothermia

Lower than normal heat in the body's core—hypothermia—subtly steals your ability to make a rational decision. Recognize it early to prevent serious problems. Or, better yet, practice prevention. The signs of hypothermia include:

▲ The "umbles": stumbling, grumbling, fumbling, mumbling.
▲ A brain dulled by the cold: dropping gear without noticing, losing direction without caring, feeling cold and doing nothing about it.
▲ Shivering that may become uncontrollable.
▲ The cessation of shivering without a return to a normal level of consciousness.

The management of hypothermia can be divided, for simplicity, into two categories: treatment for mild hypothermia and treatment for severe hypothermia.

Mild hypothermia. You can talk, eat, and shiver. Change the environment so the heat being produced internally by shivering is not lost. Get out of wet clothes and into something dry, out of wind and cold and into some kind of shelter, even if the only shelter available is in the protection of waterproof, windproof clothing. Cover your head and neck where critical heat is easily lost. Protect yourself from the cold ground. Replace fuel for the internal fire. Fluids are more important than solids to a cold person. A warm (not hot) sweet drink will add a tiny bit of heat and a lot of simple sugar for energy. Even cold fluids are better than no fluids. Stay dry and warm until you return to normal, and then you can continue the trek.

Severe hypothermia. You are semiconscious or unconscious, and you have stopped shivering. You seriously need help. Hopefully, someone will handle you with extreme gentleness. Clothing should be removed, and you should be bundled in layers of dry insulation with plenty of insulation from the ground. Hot water bottles or heat packs placed in dry socks or shirts and placed appropriately on your body—chest, palms of hands, armpits, groin—will be of benefit. Finish with a vapor barrier—a tent fly, sheet of plastic, garbage bags—something to trap any heat still left inside. The final creation is a cocoon, a "hypothermia wrap" open only to the mouth and nose.

Frostbite

When the air reaches the freezing point, your skin may not be far behind. Proper treatment of frostbite can save near-frozen tissue and reduce the extent of already-frozen tissue.

Partial thickness frostbite. Skin is pale and numb, but it moves when you press on it. Skin-to-skin warming will work as treatment, and it should begin immediately. Cover the cold body part with warm body parts. Cover your nose with your warm hand, stick your cold hand against your warm stomach, put your cold toes against the warm stomach of a friend. Do not rub the cold skin. Do not place cold skin near a hot heat source, an act that can cause damage. Take ibuprofen, if available, and drink a lot of water.

Skin that looks okay after warming is usually okay. If blisters form after warming, two things should be remembered: Leave the bubble intact. It protects the underlying tissue, and creates less chance for infection. Be careful to prevent refreezing. Blisters refreeze quickly, multiplying the damage.

Full thickness frostbite. Skin is pale and numb, hard, "woody." If refreezing is unlikely, and you have the means available, full thickness frostbite is best treated by rapid warming in water of approximately 104–108 degrees F. Too hot, and heat damage occurs. Too cold, and warming is too slow for maximum benefit. Warming is usually accomplished in thirty to forty minutes, but it is better to err on the side of caution and rewarm longer than necessary rather than less. Pain is often intense, and the strongest painkillers available should be started prior to thawing. Ibuprofen started as soon as possible seems to reduce the extent of damage to tissue. Maintain a high level of hydration. Prevention of refreezing is of paramount importance. Since thawed feet cannot and should not be walked on, you might find yourself deciding to leave hard frostbite frozen until you reach a safe place, even though immediate thawing is best for maximum benefit.

Heat Illness

Heat can cause a wide range of problems—everything from feeling hot and tired to the life-threat of heat stroke.

Heat exhaustion. With a lot of internal water sweated out, along with salt, you can feel like you are having a sudden attack of the flu: unusual fatigue, headache, nausea, dizziness. You are experiencing a volume problem—not enough water inside—and it is typically not serious, as long as you take care of the problem right away. The cure is suggested by the name of the condition: Exhaustion calls for rest, preferably in a cool, shady spot. Replace lost fluids with water, and replace lost salt by adding a pinch to a liter of water or munching salty snacks. To increase the rate of cooling, you can be wet down and fanned. If you feel drowsy, take a nap. When you feel okay, continue the adventure—but keep on drinking (see "Hydration," earlier in this section).

Heat stroke. Pushing past a minor heat problem can lead to the major illness of heat stroke in which your body is making heat faster than it is shedding it. If the heat rises too high, your brain cooks—and you die. Disorientation and bizarre personality changes are common signs. Skin turns hot and red and sometimes (but far from always) dry. You are experiencing a temperature problem—too much heat inside. Only rapid cooling will save you. Heat-retaining clothing must be removed, and you must be drenched with water. Cooling efforts, with a shortage of water, should be concentrated on the head and

---

Prevention of Frostbite

In addition to the guidelines for the prevention of hypothermia, do the following:

1. Avoid snug clothing that restricts circulation, especially on the feet and hands.
2. Wear clothing appropriate for cold weather (see "Clothing" in Before You Go).
3. Protect your skin from wind and contact with cold metal and cold gasoline.
4. Avoid alcohol and tobacco.

Prevention of Heat Illness

▲ Stay well-hydrated. Urine output should be clear and relatively copious, an indication of adequate hydration (see "Hydration," above).
▲ Munch on lightly salted snacks.
▲ Wear baggy, loosely woven clothing that allows evaporation of sweat. Keep your head shaded.
▲ Keep yourself fit. Fat encourages heat illnesses.
▲ Allow time for acclimatization when you are new to a hot environment. Go slow the first few days and avoid the hottest times of day.
▲ Beware of drugs, such as antihistamines, that increase your risk of heat illness.
▲ Rest often in the shade, especially if the humidity is high.

neck. Cold packs may be used on the palms of the hands, the soles of the feet, the head, neck, armpits, and groin. Constant fanning increases evaporation and, therefore, speeds cooling. Massage of the limbs to encourage cooler blood to return to the core is beneficial. Even in the hospital, you might come to the end of your life—and even if you return to what seems normal, the bad things high heat does to the inside of you might last for the rest of your life.

Solar Radiation

The sun shines down in a range of light that includes, on the short end of the spectrum, ultraviolet light (UV). Ultraviolet light is broken down into UVA, UVB, and UVC. UVC is almost completely blocked out by the ozone layer. Short-term overexposure to UV radiation burns skin. Prolonged exposure, over years, leads to premature skin aging and degenerative skin disorders such as cancer. First aid for sunburn includes cooling the skin, applying a moisturizer, ibuprofen for pain and inflammation, and staying out of direct sunlight. If blisters form, a doctor should be consulted. Prevention of sunburn includes hats with brims and tightly woven clothing, sunblocks such as zinc oxide, and sunscreens with a high sun protection factor.

Altitude Illness

As you ascend to higher altitudes, the amount of oxygen available in each breath you take grows lower. If you go too high too fast, problems may occur—you can get sick, and you can die. For simplicity, these problems can be divided into two categories: mild and severe.

UV Facts

- Clouds provide some shade, but very little UV protection. On a bright day with fluffy cumulus clouds dotting the sky, you can actually receive an increased dose of UVB—as much as 15 percent more—because scattered UV is reflected down to earth by the clouds. Only thick, dark rain clouds offer much UV protection.
- Summer sunshine is more harmful even though the sun in winter is closer to the earth. In summer the sun is more directly overhead. UV levels peak in most of the United States around mid-July.
- Reflection of UV light can be substantial. Grass reflects only 2–3 percent, and sand 20–30 percent. But snow and ice reflect 80–90 percent. Water can reflect 100 percent of the UV light striking its surface. Mid-morning and mid-afternoon, with the sun's rays striking at a 35–45 degree angle, water reaches the height of its reflectivity.
- Latitude changes mean UV radiation changes due to the angle of the sun's light. Equatorial locations receive the most sunshine. Skin cancer rates in Texas and Florida, according to the National Institutes of Health, are approximately twice the rates of Wisconsin and Montana.
- Wind by itself does not "burn" skin, but the combination of wind and UV radiation intensifies skin damage. Wind dries skin, removing the natural protection of urocanic acid. It irritates skin, making sunburns worse. And it cools skin, allowing longer periods of exposure without discomfort.

Mild altitude illness. Getting less oxygen than you are used to may cause a headache, unusual fatigue, nausea, loss of appetite, difficulty sleeping, unusual shortness of breath when exercising, and lassitude. The best thing to do is stop going up until your symptoms go down. Exercise lightly and drink plenty of water. Acetazolamide may be used for treatment after symptoms appear. If the symptoms do not go down within 2 days, you should.

Severe altitude illness. Serious problems may involve the brain and/or the lungs. The cause is fluid shifting out of the blood and into spaces in the head or chest. When the brain is involved, the earliest sign is usually ataxia (loss of coordination). An ataxic person cannot walk a straight line or stand straight with feet together and eyes closed. The brain problem is called High Altitude Cerebral Edema (HACE), and evidence of it also includes severe headache unrelieved by rest and medication, bizarre changes in personality, and perhaps coma. In the lungs, severe altitude illness shows up as High Altitude Pulmonary Edema (HAPE): constant shortness of breath, chest pain, at first a dry and later a productive cough. With HACE and HAPE you need to descend as soon as possible. In addition to descent, supplemental oxygen is the drug of choice. Treatment may also include the drug nifedipine for HAPE and the drug dexamethasone for HACE. Both drugs require a prescription from a physician.

Bites and Stings

Bites come from the foreparts of animals, and stings from the hindparts, just in case you were interested. Most bites and stings are no more than bothersome, but some are potentially dangerous, and some may be life-threatening.

Small insects. The little biters—mosquitoes, black flies, gnats, and such—are the most bother but the least serious (unless they happen to be a vector for disease). Bites from the little biters can often be prevented by the following: Wear clothing they cannot bite through (and lighter colors appear to offer some repellent qualities). Use insect repellents on skin. Follow the directions on the label carefully with all products, especially with products containing DEET. Use permethrin products on clothing. A wipe with a sting relief pad can ease the itching. Antihistamines, especially diphenhydramine, can reduce itching and swelling of more severe reactions. (See Appendix B for sources of information on diseases carried by little biters in the United States.)

Head nets make life with mosquitoes more pleasant and safe (NOLS/Tom Bol).

Bees and their relatives. The stinger left by honeybees should be removed as soon as possible. Any means to get it out is acceptable. Ice or cold packs on the stings from bees, wasps, yellow jackets, hornets, and fire ants will relieve pain and reduce swelling. Diphenhydramine may be given for itching and swelling.

Spiders. Shiny with an hourglass-shape almost always on the abdomen, black widows have a bite that often goes unnoticed, but local pain and redness shows up at the bite site within an hour. Severe pain from muscle cramping usually develops in the arm or leg bitten and in the abdomen and back. The pain may be incredibly severe, and fever, chills, sweating, and nausea may develop. Ice or cold packs applied to the bite site usually provide some relief. Painkilling drugs may be used, if available. Although most of the bitten recover within 24 hours, evacuation to a doctor is strongly recommended, especially for children and the elderly.

Recluse (fiddleback) spiders have a violin-shape on their back and a bite that usually produces local pain and blister formation within a few hours. A bull's-eye of discoloration often surrounds the blister. The blister ruptures, eventually, leaving a growing ulcer of skin destruction. Ice or cold packs can relieve local pain. Painkilling drugs may be useful. If the blister ruptures, treat the open wound appropriately (see "Wounds," earlier in this section). The bitten should be seen by a physician for consideration of drug treatment to minimize damage.

Scorpions. Stings from scorpions produce immediate pain soon followed by swelling. Sometimes the sting site then goes numb. Ice or cold packs will reduce pain, and diphenhydramine can be given for swelling and itching. Recovery is almost always rapid—except sometimes from the sting of *Centruroides*, a southwestern scorpion that may produce a systemic reaction characterized by unusual anxiety, sweating, salivation, gastrointestinal distress, and, most importantly, respiratory distress. No specific first aid is useful for *Centruroides* stings, and immediate evacuation should take place.

Ticks. The little, eight-legged tick, in numerous species, may carry diseases that it can pass to humans. Insect repellents repel ticks, and ticks crawling around on your skin do not transmit diseases until they dig in and feed for hours to days, the time dependent on the species. Careful tick checks should be performed at least twice a day in tick-infected country, and early removal of imbedded ticks prevents the transmission of many diseases. They should be removed gently with tweezers, without excess squeezing, by taking hold of the tick as near to the skin as possible and pulling straight out. Any other removal method increases the risk of germ transmission. Wash the wound. A swipe with an antiseptic may be useful. Watch for signs of illness—rash, fever, flu-like symptoms—which should send you to a doctor as soon as possible.

Snakes. A pit viper (rattlesnake, water moccasin, copperhead) bites with either or both retractable fangs, producing immediate local pain and swelling within approximately fifteen minutes. Blister formation and discoloration usually occur, and may lead to local skin destruction. The bitten often report lip-tingling and a funny taste in their mouth within an hour or so. Muscle twitching may result. Death is rare.

Coral snakes, with relatively dull fangs, have to gnaw a few moments to deposit venom. Burning pain at the bite site is often followed by pain, tingling, or numbness extending up from the bite—but these signs and symptoms make take up to 12 hours to develop. Serious systemic manifestations include difficulty speaking, swallowing, seeing, and breathing. Bites are far less common, and far more dangerous.

After any snakebite, follow this advice:
1. Get away from the snake.
2. Remain as calm as possible.
3. Remove anything that might restrict circulation, such as rings, before swelling occurs.
4. If you have a negative-pressure venom extraction device, use it as soon as possible. Rapid use may remove a significant amount of venom.
5. Gently wash the bite site.
6. Splint the bitten arm or leg, and keep the bite site on a level with the heart.
7. Find a doctor.
8. Do not use cold packs, tourniquets, cutting-and-sucking, or electrical shocks.

> "We carry with us the wonders
> we seek without us."
> *Sir Thomas Browne*

Camp Hygiene

You might think the great majority of germs that cause disease in humans lurk in the wilderness, an inherent part of the wildland. Not so. In fact, in most cases, the contrary is true: The germs hitched a free ride into the wilderness with you or some other unwary bipedal primate. The presence of humans, even if only for a short while, has built most of the community of disease possibilities. We, in other words, spread the germs to other members of our group, and leave some behind for the next trekker.

Hand washing. Nothing prevents the spread of disease more aggressively than hand washing. Under a microscope, your skin, especially your hands, looks like an aerial view of southern Utah: canyons and mesas, cracks and fissures. Microbes are often wedged firmly into the low spots. Some of these microbes are friendly, but some can make you severely sick. Bad germs can accumulate rapidly after bowel movements, and they congregate most thickly under fingernails and in the deeper fissures of fingertips.

Washing your hands, even with detergents, does not remove all the flora living there, but it does significantly reduce the chance of contamination. Hands end up the cleanest when you use hot water and soap, and scrub up until you have a thick lather. Concentrate the lathering on your fingertips. Then rinse and dry. Drying is important because it removes germs that are not killed in the washing process.

You can get your hands clean enough with cold water and a germicidal soap. And, although you need a scrubbing now and then to remove dirt, you can also get by with a hand sanitizer, a product that allows you to squirt a dab on your hands and rub it in to kill germs.

Dishes, pots and pans. Dishes, cups, and eating utensils should be washed every day. Pots and pans brought to high heat during food prep can go for several days between washings. When you do wash cookware, do the following: Remove as much of the visible food scraps as possible. Use hot, soapy water and an abrasive pad. Rinse in hot water and wipe dry with a clean cloth. Or you can rinse in cold water with chlorine added. It does not take much chlorine. If the water smells faintly of chlorine, there is enough in the rinse water.

Food handling. Contamination can be further reduced by pouring all food, including trail mix, out of bags instead of reaching in for it. If someone in your group is already sick, that person should be allowed to skip kitchen duty until he or she is healthy again. Germs proliferate in old, cooked food, and that makes leftovers a risk. Leftovers are best left uneaten and packed out. But, okay, maybe once in a while you want to finish last night's dinner. Add a little water and bring the food to high heat. Let it re-cook for several minutes, stirring occasionally to prevent an unpalatable burned mess.

Sharing. Nice people are willing to share, but they may be passing around more than their water bottle. Do not drink from someone else's personal cup or bottle, or use their unwashed spoon. Keep your lip balm and your toothbrush to yourself. Do not share your bandanna. Do not let someone else finish your half-eaten granola bar.

Human waste. For the safety of you and your group, and future trekkers, manage your fecal matter and urine in a manner appropriate for the local environment and according to the specifics of the Leave No Trace program (see "Leave No Trace" earlier in this section).

For Women Only
by Annette McGivney, Southwest editor for Backpacker

As a woman, you might find yourself having thoughts, at least more often than men, about the following concerns:

Bears and menstruation. In two separate attacks on one evening in August 1967—"the night of the grizzly"—two women campers died. One had been menstruating. What ensued, to the detriment of bears and women, was the rapid spread of a misconception that associated bear attacks with menstruation. The fact: That was the only known attack in U.S. history by a bear on a woman having her period. "It's a myth," says Steven P. French, M.D., research director of the Yellowstone Grizzly Foundation. "There is no scientific evidence showing bears (grizzly or black) are attracted to menstrual odor." In fact, French thinks, with his tongue only slightly stuck in his cheek, "You're at a higher risk if you have testicles because men take more risks and use poorer judgment." So there is no reason to stay out of bear country just because you are menstruating. You should, however, double bag in plastic all soiled tampons and pads to minimize waste odors that may make bears and other animals curious. Hang the bags with your other trash, well away from your tent and out of bear reach. If you want to minimize smells on your person, wear unscented tampons instead of sanitary napkins. Menstrual fluid is odorless inside the body.

A pain in the crotch. Going without a shower for days on end has more than just aesthetic implications. It could nurture a case of *Candida*, otherwise known as a yeast infection, one of the most common afflictions to strike women on extended wilderness trips. The possible causes, in addition to poor hygiene in the nether regions, include lowered immune response brought on by the unusual stress of toting a pack, recent or current use of antibiotics or birth control pills, and vaginal cuts or abrasions from tampon use or intercourse. Yeast makes its presence known with a burning and/or itching in the vagina. It could also cause a redness, soreness, and swelling in the vaginal area, and an irritating pain on urination. But, contrary to popular belief, a yeast infection does not always produce a visible vaginal discharge.

A variety of over-the-counter creams, tablets, and suppositories provide the foundation of treatment. Buy a product that contains at least one of these active ingredients: butoconazole, clotrimazole, miconazole, or triconazole. Three days of treatment usually provides the best initial response with less chance of a quick return of the yeast. While topical prescription creams are generally no more effective than the over-the-counter variety, there is a prescription pill that can work wonders. Fluconazole (a single dose of 150 mg taken orally) typically offers quick resolution of the problem and should be considered a worthy addition to a wilderness first-aid kit. But the best treatment, of course, is prevention. Wash the vaginal and perianal area daily. Allow the crotch to air dry by wearing loose-fitting clothing—or none at all. Opt for cotton underpants if you are infection-prone—synthetics are less absorbent and promote the growth of bacteria.

How to pee in the woods. When it comes to taking a leak, guys have it easy. Just aim and fire. No cold buns. No splatter factor. Women are at disadvantage in this department, but there are things you can do to improve the projected outcome. Here are three different methods:

1. Find a place where you can sit with your feet propped up: two rocks close together, a rock and a log, or whatever. This keeps you relaxed and your boots dry.
2. Find a crack where you can stand and pee—between two rocks or logs, for example.
3. Find a soft patch of earth and dig a shallow hole (to expose absorbent dirt) with the heel of your boot. Squat with your arms extended out in front to counterbalance yourself or hang on to a branch or rock to aid in relaxation. Cover the christened spot by kicking the dirt and duff back where it was.

The peeing process can also be made easier by wearing a skirt or pants with a "split pee" zippered crotch. And if you do splatter, do not worry about it. Boots that smell like a stadium urinal pose no health risks.

A happy bladder. If you are susceptible to urinary tract infections, take special precautions to prevent one on treks. Drink plenty of water to flush your system and stay well hydrated. Be sure to relax and empty your bladder completely when urinating. In your first-aid kit carry an antibiotic for treating urinary tract infections.

Refresh your tresses. If you are one of those whose hair gets oily quickly, backpacking for days without washing can be a head-spinning experience. To help get rid of the grease when soap and water is not convenient, use cornstarch. Massage a small amount of the powder into your hair and scalp to absorb the oil, then comb it out to avoid the dandruff look. Cornstarch also works well to untangle hair.

Rub-a-dub-dub. Many civilized traditions can be abandoned on wilderness trips but cleaning your nether regions should not be one of them. Good hygiene guards against yeast infections, and minimizes odors (especially if you are menstruating), and it just helps you to maintain that "fresh feeling." Wear unscented tampons, if possible, instead of maxi-pads. Wash your crotch regularly with unscented wet wipes, and if menstrual flow is heavy, you may also want to bring along a little squirt bottle to serve as a backcountry bidet. Bring changes of clean underwear and/or wash your undies frequently.

PART 4
Coming Home

> "There is no cure for birth or death,
> save to enjoy the interval."
> *Santayana*

Home is where the heart is, and maybe you left at least a part of yours behind. After a meal of fresh food and a reunion with loved ones, after a hot shower and a bottle of cold beer, be prepared for a form of depression. Be prepared for a period of reintegration. Your bed may feel too soft, the air within four walls too close, the ring of the telephone too disturbing. These feelings are not bad. Neither are they good. They just are. They are as much a part of the journey as the first moment you decided to step out on a trek. There are memories that will last your lifetime—I guarantee it. You have learned things that will soften and enliven and, perhaps, empower the rest of your days.

If you kept a journal—and I have trouble imagining a trek without one—reread it soon. Relive the days before your recollections of the specifics start to fade. Scribble notes to yourself that will only come with hindsight. Offer recommendations to yourself for your next trek. Add points to remember to your maps. Wallow in nostalgia. These things are also a part of the journey.

From a practical aspect, there are activities well-suited to the post-trekker. There are healthy ways to store your gear and clothing, and, conversely, there are unhealthy ways. You want everything to last as long as possible, and you want it to be ready for the next time. Some particular suggestions include the following:

▲ Do not store anything wet. Mildew will compromise the integrity of anything.
▲ Do not dry (or store) anything synthetic in direct sunlight. Ultraviolet light deteriorates most artificial fibers.

Home is where the heart is (NOLS/Tom Bol).

- ▲ Do not store anything dirty. Scrub the pots and pans. Wash the clothes. Wipe out the tent and pack with a damp sponge. Clean and oil the leather boots. Empty fuel from the stove, and clean the fuel ports.
- ▲ Do not store your sleeping bag stuffed. At least place it in a large, breathable bag that allows partial fluffing.
- ▲ Do not put off making repairs, sealing seams, replacing what needs replacing, and righting wrongs.

The thoughts, the suggestions, the recommendations, the directions you have been reading are merely words. I do not know what you will do, and I do not care what you will do—because neither of those things matter. I do hope, however, that you will take your trek, that you defend and protect the wildlands, that you walk in peace whenever you can, that you live your dreams. And, in closing, this might be a fine time to remind you of the words of William Gilbert: "Look for knowledge not in books but in things themselves." Happy trails!

APPENDIX A

Resources

Federal Land Management Agencies

Bureau of Land Management (BLM)
1849 C Street NW
Washington, DC 20240
(202) 208-3801
www.blm.gov

National Park Service (NPS)
1849 C Street NW
Washington, DC 20240
(202) 208-6843
www.nps.gov

U.S. Forest Service (USFS)
201 14th Street SW
Washington, DC 20024
(202) 205-8333
www.fs.fed.us

Map Makers

DeLorme: (800) 561-5105, *www.delorme.com*
International Map Trade Association: *www.maptrade.org*
Online maps: *www.topozone.com, www.maps.com, www.trails.com*
Trails Illustrated and National Geographic: (800) 962-1643
   http://maps.nationalgeographic.com/trails/maps.cfm
USGS Map Sales, Federal Center, Box 25286, Denver, CO 80225.
   See the USGS website, *http://mcmcweb.er.usgs.gov/topomaps*, for a listing of
   businesses that sell USGS quad maps.

Happy trails! (NOLS/Tom Bol)

Conservation Organizations/Hiking Clubs

Adirondack Mountain Club (ADK)
    814 Goggins Road
    Lake George, NY 12845
    (518) 668-4447
    (800) 395-8080
    www.adk.org

American Hiking Society
    1422 Fenwick Lane
    Silver Spring, MD 20910
    (301) 565-6704
    www.americanhiking.org

Appalachian Mountain Club (AMC)
    5 Joy Street
    Boston, MA 02108
    (617) 523-0636
    www.outdoors.org

Colorado Mountain Club
    710 Tenth Street, No. 200
    Golden, CO 80401
    (303) 279-3080
    www.cmc.org

Green Mountain Club
    4711 Waterbury-Stowe Road
    Waterbury Center, VT 05677
    (802) 244-7037
    www.greenmountainclub.org

Idaho Conservation League
    P.O. Box 844
    Boise, ID 83701
    (208) 345-6933
    www.wildIDAHO.org

Leave No Trace Center for Outdoor Ethics
P.O. Box 997
Boulder, CO 80306-9816
(800) 332-4100
www.LNT.org

National Parks and Conservation Association
1300 19th Street NW
Washington, DC 20036
(800) 628-7275
www.npca.org

The Nature Conservancy (TNC)
4245 North Fairfax Drive, Suite 100
Arlington, VA 22203-1606
(703) 841-5300
www.nature.org

Sierra Club
85 Second Street, Second Floor
San Francisco, CA 94105-3441
(415) 977-5500
www.sierraclub.org

Southern Utah Wilderness Alliance (SUWA)
1471 South 1100 East
Salt Lake City, UT 84105
(801) 486-3161
www.suwa.org

The Wilderness Society
900 17th Street NW
Washington, DC 20006-2596
(800) THE-WILD
www.wilderness.org

Wilderness Education

National Outdoor Leadership School (NOLS)
284 Lincoln Street
Lander, WY 82520-2848
(307) 332-5300
www.nols.edu

SOLO (Stonehearth Open Learning Opportunities)
P.O. Box 3150, Tasker Hill
Conway, NH 03818
(603) 447-6711
www.stonehearth.com

Wilderness Medical Associates
RFD 2, Box 890
Bryant Pond, ME 04219
(888) 945-3633
www.wildmed.com

Wilderness Medicine Institute of the National Outdoor Leadership School (WMI)
284 Lincoln Street
Lander, WY 82520-2848
(307) 332-7800
www.wmi.nols.edu/

Weather

National Weather Service: *weather.noaa.gov/weather/ccus.html*
Wind chill index: *www.nws.noaa.gov/om/windchill/*
U.S. Forest Service National Avalanche Center: *www.avalanche.org*

International Travel

Centers for Disease Control (CDC) International Traveler's Hotline:
    (877) FYI-TRIP
International Association for Medical Assistance to Traveler's (IAMAT)
    417 Center Street
    Lewiston, NY 14092
    (716) 754-4883
U.S. State Department Travel Warnings and Consular Information Sheets:
    travel.state.gov/travel_warnings.html

APPENDIX B
Bibliography

Berger, Karen. *Everyday Wisdom: 1001 Expert Tips for Hikers.* Seattle: The Mountaineers Books/*Backpacker* magazine, 1997.

———. *Hiking the Triple Crown: How to Hike America's Longest Trails.* Seattle: The Mountaineers Books, 2001.

———. *More Everyday Wisdom.* Seattle: The Mountaineers Books/*Backpacker* magazine, 2002.

Burns, Bob, and Mike Burns. *Wilderness Navigation: Finding Your Way Using Map, Compass, Altimeter, and GPS.* Seattle: The Mountaineers Books, 1999.

Cox, Stephen, and Kris Fulsaas, eds. *Mountaineering: The Freedom of the Hills.* Seattle: The Mountaineers Books, 2003.

Culture Shock! series. Kuperard, Number 9 Hampstead West, 244 Iverson Road, London NW6 2HL. A series of books detailing cultural differences in many countries.

Fleming, June. *Staying Found: The Complete Map and Compass Handbook.* 3rd ed. Seattle: The Mountaineers Books, 2001.

Getchell, Annie. *The Essential Outdoor Gear Manual: Equipment Care & Repair for Outdoorspeople.* Camden, Maine: Ragged Mountain Press, 1995.

Gray, Melissa, and Buck Tilton. *Cooking the One Burner Way.* 2nd ed. Guilford, Conn.: The Globe Pequot Press, 2000.

Hampton, Bruce, and David Cole. *Soft Paths: How to Enjoy the Wilderness without Harming It.* Mechanicsburg, Pa.: Stackpole Books, 1995.

Harvey, Mark. *The NOLS Wilderness Guide.* New York: Simon & Schuster, 1999.

Jacobson, Cliff. *The Basic Essentials of Map and Compass.* Guilford, Conn.: The Globe Pequot Press, 1988.

Lanza, Michael. *Ultimate Guide to Backcountry Travel.* Boston: Appalachian Mountain Club Books, 1999.

Letham, Lawrence. *GPS Made Easy: Using Global Positioning Systems in the Outdoors.* 3rd ed. Seattle: The Mountaineers Books, 2001.

Lindgren, Louise. *Sew and Repair Your Outdoor Gear.* Seattle: The Mountaineers Books, 1989.

Long, John, and Michael Hodgson. *The Complete Hiker.* Camden, Maine: Ragged Mountain Press, 2000.

McGivney, Annette. *Leave No Trace: A Guide to the New Wilderness Etiquette.* Seattle: The Mountaineers Books/*Backpacker* magazine, 2003.

Miller, Dorcas. *Backcountry Cooking: From Pack to Plate in 10 Minutes.* Seattle: The Mountaineers Books/*Backpacker* magazine, 1998.

Musnick, David, and Mark Pierce. *Conditioning for Outdoor Fitness: A Comprehensive Training Guide.* Seattle: The Mountaineers Books, 1999.

Renner, Jeff. *Lightning Strikes.* Seattle: The Mountaineers Books, 2001.

Ross, Cindy, and Todd Gladfelter. *A Hiker's Companion: 12,000 Miles of Trail-Tested Wisdom.* Seattle: The Mountaineers Books, 1993.

———. *Kids in the Wild: A Family Guide to Outdoor Recreation.* Seattle: The Mountaineers Books, 1995.

Schad, Jerry, and David Moser, eds. *Wilderness Basics: The Complete Handbook for Hikers and Backpackers.* 2nd ed. Seattle: The Mountaineers Books, 1992.

Smith, David. *Backcountry Bear Basics: The Definitive Guide to Avoiding Unpleasant Encounters.* Seattle: The Mountaineers Books, 1997.

Steele, Peter. *Backcountry Medical Guide.* 2nd ed. Seattle: The Mountaineers Books, 1999.

Strauss, Robert. *Adventure Trekking: A Handbook for Independent Travelers.* Seattle: The Mountaineers Books, 1996.

Tilton, Buck. *The Basic Essentials of Avalanche Safety.* Guilford, Conn.: The Globe Pequot Press, 1992.

———. *The Basic Essentials of Rescue from the Backcountry.* Guilford, Conn.: The Globe Pequot Press, 1990.

———. *Don't Get Bitten: The Dangers of Bites and Stings.* Seattle: The Mountaineers Books, 2003.

Tilton, Buck, and Rick Bennett. *Don't Get Sick: The Hidden Dangers of Camping and Hiking.* Seattle: The Mountaineers Books, 2002.

Tilton, Buck, and Frank Hubbell. *Medicine for the Backcountry: A Practical Guide to Wilderness First Aid.* 3rd ed. Guilford, Conn.: The Globe Pequot Press, 1999.

Tremper, Bruce. *Staying Alive in Avalanche Terrain.* Seattle: The Mountaineers Books, 2001.

Van Tilburg, Christopher. *Emergency Survival: A Pocket Guide.* Seattle: The Mountaineers Books, 2001.

Weiss, Eric. *Wilderness 911: A Step-by-Step Guide for Medical Emergencies and Improvised Care in the Backcountry.* Seattle: The Mountaineers Books/*Backpacker* magazine, 1998.

Wilkerson, James A., ed. *Medicine for Mountaineering and Other Wilderness Activities.* 5th ed. Seattle: The Mountaineers Books, 2001.

Index

About the Author

Freelance writer Buck Tilton is the longest-serving contributing editor to *Backpacker* magazine. He has written more than 1000 magazine articles, and this book brings his published titles to twenty-four in number. In love with the wildlands, he has trekked—by foot, canoe, and sea kayak—for too many thousands of miles to ever remember. In 1990, he cofounded the Wilderness Medicine Institute, a part of the National Outdoor Leadership School since 1999. Born in South Carolina, he went west with all the young men, got an M.S. in Experiential Education, and has enjoyed more than thirty years of teaching and writing. He lives in Lander, Wyoming.

THE MOUNTAINEERS, founded in 1906, is a nonprofit outdoor activity and conservation club, whose mission is "to explore, study, preserve, and enjoy the natural beauty of the outdoors{4ell}" Based in Seattle, Washington, the club is now the third-largest such organization in the United States, with seven branches throughout Washington State.

The Mountaineers sponsors both classes and year-round outdoor activities in the Pacific Northwest, which include hiking, mountain climbing, ski-touring, snowshoeing, bicycling, camping, kayaking, nature study, sailing, and adventure travel. The club's conservation division supports environmental causes through educational activities, sponsoring legislation, and presenting informational programs. All club activities are led by skilled, experienced instructors, who are dedicated to promoting safe and responsible enjoyment and preservation of the outdoors.

If you would like to participate in these organized outdoor activities or the club's programs, consider a membership in The Mountaineers. For information and an application, write or call The Mountaineers, Club Headquarters, 300 Third Avenue West, Seattle, WA 98119; 206-284-6310. You can also visit the club's website at *www.mountaineers.org* or contact The Mountaineers via email at *clubmail@mountaineers.org*.

The Mountaineers Books, an active, nonprofit publishing program of the club, produces guidebooks, instructional texts, historical works, natural history guides, and works on environmental conservation. All books produced by The Mountaineers Books fulfill the club's mission.

Send or call for our catalog of more than 500 outdoor titles:

The Mountaineers Books
1001 SW Klickitat Way, Suite 201
Seattle, WA 98134
800-553-4453
mbooks@mountaineersbooks.org
www.mountaineersbooks.org

BACKPACKER
The Magazine Of Wilderness Travel

33 East Minor Street
Emmaus, PA 18098
800-666-3434
www.backpacker.com
The mission of Backpacker magazine is to provide accurate, useful, in-depth,
and engaging information about wilderness recreation in North America.

The Mountaineers Books is proud to be a corporate sponsor of The Leave No Trace Center for Outdoor Ethics, whose mission is to promote and inspire responsible outdoor recreation through education, research, and partnerships. The Leave No Trace program is focused specifically on human-powered (nonmotorized) recreation.

Leave No Trace strives to educate visitors about the nature of their recreational impacts, as well as offer techniques to prevent and minimize such impacts. Leave No Trace is best understood as an educational and ethical program, not as a set of rules and regulations.

For more information, visit www.LNT.org, or call 800-332-4100.